NET
75—

signed
(cond. noted)

FOUNTAINS ABBEY

Herbert Whone
May 1990

Dedication

To my youngest daughter Hannah, on her 18th birthday.

Stand on this level turf until you hear
The echo of the voices that are gone,
This cloistered peace, this loveliness austere
And tranquil, this calm vision of white stone
Once spoke: the broken accents murmur on,
Like truth imprisoned in a cobwebbed tome
Or martyrs preaching in a catacomb.

from the poem 'Fountains Abbey'
E. K. Ellis, 1948

FOUNTAINS ABBEY

Photographs taken and
Text chosen by
HERBERT WHONE

With a Foreword by
THE LORD GIBSON
Chairman of the National Trust 1977-1986

SMITH SETTLE
1987

First published in 1987 by
SMITH SETTLE
Ilkley Road, Otley,
West Yorkshire LS21 3JP

Copyright © HERBERT WHONE 1987

All rights reserved. No part of this book may be reproduced, stored in a retrieval system, or transmitted, in any form or by any means, electronic, mechanical, photocopying, recording or otherwise, without the prior permission of the publishers.

ISBN Paperback 1 870071 08 5
      Hardback   1 870071 07 7

Designed, printed and bound by
SMITH SETTLE
Ilkley Road, Otley
West Yorkshire LS21 3JP

About the Author

Although trained as a musician, Mr. Whone is an artist in the broadest sense, having made a reputation during his life as a violinist, teacher, painter, writer and photographer. And behind, sustaining all, he says, has been his interest in religion, either outwardly in church buildings, or inwardly in their symbolism and in each man's spiritual quest. This book on Fountains Abbey is an extension of this interest.

Born in Bingley, Yorkshire in 1925, he graduated at the Manchester University and Royal College of Music, and after a war-time period in the RAF continued his studies in Paris, where his interest in art began. He was a member of the BBC Symphony Orchestra, and later in the 1950s became deputy-leader of the Scottish National Orchestra. Whilst in Scotland his exhibitions of paintings of the Glasgow scene were widely acknowledged. In 1965 he left full-time orchestral playing and returned to his native Yorkshire to take a teaching post in the Music Department of the Huddersfield Polytechnic. Between 1965 and 1970 he held shows of paintings of the West Riding landscape in local galleries and in public Art Galleries.

In the early 1970s Mr. Whone wrote three books on music published by Gollancz, and did radio recitals. At the same time his fascination for the landscape of his childhood resulted in the publication of *The Essential West Riding*, 150 photographs taken during his walks, along with text from West Riding authors (re-issued, 1987, in a new format by the publishers of this present work). Following this he wrote a book on Church symbolism, *Church, Monastery, Cathedral* (Compton Russell Element) which he describes as a visitor's hand-book.

Since 1980, Mr. Whone has published a collection of what he calls philosophical ditties — *Nursery Rhymes for Adult Children* (Tallis Press), and has held an exhibition of photographs and drawings of trees in the Harrogate Art Gallery and elsewhere. Latterly, he has been engaged in studying Fountains Abbey, and in the season, is a voluntary guide for the National Trust. His involvement with music continues — he is currently leader of the York Guildhall Orchestra. His other full-time occupation, not quite over, Mr. Whone says, has been the bringing up of five children. Thanks to an understanding wife he looks back on his life of art, religion and domesticity with pleasure and gratitude.

Contents

As the book contains much overlapping of word and picture, it is not possible to give an exact 'contents'. The broad indication below applies, if anything, more to the text.

Page 1   The Cistercians.

16   The lay-brothers.

22   The beginnings of the Abbey.

42   The masons and builders.

46   Chapter house business, colonisation, the fire.

61   The church.

77   Guest houses and dormitory arrangements.

88   The remaining cloister buildings: treasury, warming house, refectory, kitchen.

112   Everyday life — accounts, stores, sanitary arrangements.

132   The infirmary.

143   Charters and endowments.

150   Sheep farming and granges.

157   Historical letters and documents.

175   Huby's tower.

178   The Dissolution.

195   Glossary.

198   Bibliography.

199   Index to Photographs.

         Map.

Acknowledgements

Mary Mauchline for the initial inspiration to revere the Abbey of St. Mary of Fountains.

English Heritage and National Trust for permission to take photographs freely throughout the Abbey.

Alan Quicke, of the Huddersfield Polytechnic Library, for translating a number of Latin texts, viz. those on pages 18, 19, 29, 30, 31, 39, 51, 53, 55, 58, 94, 108, 118, 119, 144, 151, 168.

The publishers who allowed me to use work of their respective authors. They are named at the back of the book.

Foreword

Fountains Abbey approached from the east along the valley from Studley Royal is surely one of the most beautiful places on earth.

As the visitor makes his way along the path by the canals laid out in the 18th century, the hills on either side set with temples in the classical taste, the great mediaeval abbey stands as the climax of his journey — a monument to the faith of the Middle Ages at the end of a passage through a Claudian landscape inspired by the pagan ideal. The impression is unforgettable and it is a matter for rejoicing that abbey and valley have now been brought together in the hands of The National Trust which is to look after them for ever.

Visitors who have enjoyed the rare experience of Fountains Abbey and Studley Royal will find great pleasure in this collection of pictures and literary quotations brought together by Mr. Whone. It is a delightful anthology, which entertains as well as informs, and all those who love Fountains are greatly in Mr. Whone's debt.

APRIL 1987

Introduction

I am one of many people who have fallen under the spell of Fountains Abbey, or more properly the Abbey of St. Mary of Fountains. What that spell is, it is difficult to say: all I know is that a visit somehow leaves me with a prevailing sense of peace. Perhaps it lies in the contemplative nature of the Cistercian order. If men have sought the inner mysteries of the spirit there for over four hundred years, it may not be surprising that something of the wisdom they have achieved lingers on in the air and in the stones. Of course, any creation of man, humble or exalted, bears within it and transmits the essential stamp and intention of its creator. But here — in this place more than any other I know — is peace.

Despite this, we may see from the historical evidence in the book that the monk's world, though set in pleasant pastures, was an imperfect one. Along with his inevitable soul struggle, he was to some extent at the mercy of and dependent upon the outside world. Fires, famines, greedy kings, incursions by Scots armies, pestilences, criminal attacks, sheep scab, and latterly the decline of values within the order itself, were to intrude upon that peace. Nevertheless, if we are wise, we will look behind all these disturbances and aim to recall the essential life of the Abbey, the Opus Dei or worship, going on with unfailing regularity day by day, and building up that contemplative ethos we sense today.

It is so easy, in walking around the shell of an abbey such as Fountains, to come away with only a vague impression of ruins. Who can visualise the manifold aspects of its daily life, the endless nocturnal processions from dormitory to church, the chantings, the rituals in the refectory, the meetings in the chapter house, the constant comings and goings of guests and commodities through the gates, the movements to and from the outlying granges, and the endless changes in its history? It is difficult enough to imagine it habitable only, with a roof and furnishings! I see ample evidence of this as I take people around in my capacity of volunteer guide for the National Trust. A guide book is of course indispensable, and no one could do better than follow the excellent one currently available at the entrance to the Abbey.* To such a guide, this book is an extension and a supplement. It is not an architectural or a historical treatise, but a human experience — an attempt to convey, by photographs taken in all sorts of weathers, by contemporary documents relative to its history, and by words of later writers who have understood it intimately, something of that lost life. It is impossible, I know, but it is an attempt from the heart. To the more recent writers, from the middle of the last century when the beauty of Fountains was being discovered, to the present day, I am more than grateful. I would like to think I am embodying their works of love in my own present work.

I am not an architectural or a historical specialist in the academic sense, but I have a lifetime of study of ancient monuments, especially churches, behind me, plus much professional involvement in various aspects of art. In the question of dating and identification, therefore, with specialist opinion constantly shifting, I can only go by the latest findings. For instance, in the latest edition of the guide book to which I have referred, it has been thought advisable not to describe the remains which lie on the south side of the River Skell as the 'bakehouse and malthouse', but to substitute the names 'northern and southern industrial buildings'. This is because recent excavations have indicated that the site of the bakehouse had a variety of functions, being in the 12th century a large aisled hall which underwent many modifications, later a woolhouse with its fulling mill in one corner, and latterly a smithy where the furnaces,

* 'Fountains Abbey' by R. Gilyard-Beer, printed under the auspices of English Heritage.

it is thought, once heated coppers in a room above. But because there is still doubt, and it is the furnaces or ovens we see, I have decided in the photographs to retain the traditional name along with the new one. Similarly there may be slight discrepancies in dates, as with the fire of 1147, which specialists now tell us took place in 1146. Those who wish to have the full picture must consult the guide book. Also, some of the photographs are of, and taken from, parts of the Abbey closed to the public; but here too, things are in constant change. Restoration will soon make some of them accessible to visitors, and excavations will reveal more and more secrets as time goes on.

As to the photographs themselves, they were taken in the first place for reasons of beauty or interest — the idea of a book emerged later. It was a question then of joining words and image in a happy marriage, so that good photographs did not have to be abandoned. The reader will realise that despite its overall plan and sequential development, a one-to-one correspondence between picture and text was neither possible nor desirable in a book of this sort. For those interested, I have used one camera, a Praktica MTL 3, and the film used was generally FP4. Many visits were necessary to arrive at this collection, because as all photographers will understand, successful pictures are hard to come by. In the drawings I do, poetic licence operates immediately, but the eye of the camera cannot lie and pictures present themselves, more often than not, when least expected. I should know, as I have been taking photographs since the age of thirteen! It may be asked by some why there are so many snow scenes. I would answer that I am simply being realistic — our northern winter is a long one, and the warming house fire was lit almost six months of the monks' year. Also, not only does snow beautify, but it often shows up architectural detail in an unexpected and delicate way.

As to the documents, it will be realised that they are mostly translations from Latin — the one or two that are not are from the early 16th century. I am grateful for the kind help of the keepers of the books in various reference libraries, especially Mr Barr at the York Minster Library and Mr Capel at the Harrogate Reference Library. Mr Capel kindly checked the ms. in its later stages for me and also translated the prayer on page 146. I am also grateful to Mr Maurice Turner of Knaresborough for a few helpful points on deeds, in the glossary. And finally whilst on the subject of text and documents, I would like to draw attention to the fact that 400 years is a long period of time for any rule or practice to be maintained, and I ask readers to have a flexible mind and to consider the changes that history within and without the Abbey must have brought about. Some conflicting statements are easily accounted for by the passage of time. Equally, there are things we are never likely to know with any degree of accuracy. How did the monks fare during the Black Death? What was the exact use put to the infirmary buildings? What was the population of the Abbey at any given time? At what date was fish admitted to the menu? For these, and many other questions large and small, there is no evidence. We can only conjecture and draw parallels.

Finally I would like to make it clear that I have chosen the texts without any side or judgement: they represent different facets of the story of Fountains and of the Cistercian religious life. I believe only that true religion has a continual theme, the re-uniting of the soul to its spiritual source, which we call God — the birth of the Christ within. It is for this reason that the book opens with a statement of man's inner quest by St. Bernard. I respect this perennial message in whatever form or in whatever time it occurs.

I would like to thank Mr Dave Sweeney, National Heritage site manager of the restoration work, who patiently guided one familiar with the earth level up the scaffolding for bird's-eye views, and also Mr Alan Cuckston who drew my attention to one of the rare fragments of music to survive from the Abbey, an excerpt from which is on page 212. Mr Cuckston directed performances by the Ripon College Singers of some of these fragments, and my cousin John Whone's Praetorius Ensemble did transcribed versions on the site in 1973. My thanks are also due to Dr A. J. Moyes of Leeds who painstakingly checked the galley-proofs and advised on a number of architectural issues, and to Mr Philip Tennant (Tennant Brown photographers, Harrogate) who sensitively prepared some of the enlargements for printing.

My indebtedness to particular individuals is noted under 'Acknowledgements' and to publishers in the list at the back of the book; and all of us should be grateful for the thoughtful guardianship of the National Trust and the restoration work of English Heritage, which together ensure the preservation of Fountains Abbey for future generations. I should also remind readers that a visit to Fountains Abbey embraces the beautiful 18th century grounds of Studley Royal, with its ornamental gardens, trees and deer park — a feast indeed. But my supreme acknowledgement is to the countless beings, monks and otherwise, who kept this extraordinary monument in working existence for 400 years. I bow before the Spirit within which moved them all to do so. It is these factors together, the human dedication and the quickening Spirit, which allow me along with hundreds of thousands of visitors to feel refreshed and sustained in an age of difficult transition where faith has not quite found its next appropriate expression and habitation.

HERBERT WHONE
Harrogate

Add to this the fact that the desire for earthly things (all of which are destined to perish) increases the darkness of the soul, so that in the soul that lives in such desires nothing can be seen any more on any side, save the pallid face and the image, as it were, of death. Why does not this soul, since it is immortal, love the immortal and the undying things which are like itself that thus she might appear as she truly is and live as she was made to live? But no, she takes her delight in knowing and seeking what is contrary to her nature and, by living in this manner that is so far beneath her, placing herself on the level of perishing things and becoming like them, she blackens the whiteness of her immortality with the pitch of this familiarity with death. For it is not to be wondered at that the desire of material things makes the immortal soul like unto mortal beings, and unlike to the immortal. 'He that toucheth pitch' says the Wise Man, 'shall be defiled with it'. The soul that seeks to rest and take its fill of delight in mortal things puts on mortality like a garment, and yet the garment of immortality is not put off, but discoloured by the arrival of this likeness of death.

....

....

That which is thine, and really thine, is not to be found here: it is something totally different from these: for it is eternal, and of eternity. Why do you force your soul to take on the impress of an alien form, or rather an alien deformity? Yea, indeed, that which she loves to possess, she fears to lose. Now fear is a kind of colour. It stains our liberty and, discolouring it, conceals it, and, at the same time, makes it unlike to itself. How much more worthy of her origin would it have been if only this soul had desired nothing, feared nothing and thereby have defended its own liberty, remaining in her native strength and beauty.

St. Bernard of Clairvaux 1091-1153: as translated in 'Thomas Merton on St. Bernard', 1980

At the end of the eleventh century the Cluniacs relaxed from a strict observance of St. Benedict's Rule. And in 1098, St. Robert, Abbot of Molesmes, founded a monastery in the middle of the swampy forest at Cîteaux (Diocese of Langres) to reform the Rule. This new monastery really began to prosper only in 1112 when Bernard, a young nobleman of the region, entered it with a few companions. When Bernard died in 1153, the Cistercian order had 343 monasteries and before the end of the century, 530. St. Bernard, *the* spirit and power of the order, organized the Second Crusade in 1147 and was the arbiter of European politics as well as Christianity's chief officer. His determination to comply with absolute strictness to St. Benedict's Rule had important spiritual, social, economic, and technical consequences.

St. Bernard and his companions withdrew from the world in which this taste for life and luxury, even among the Cluniacs, had replaced the love of God. To protect them from every worldly temptation, the order required its monks to rid themselves of every luxury and retire to the forests. Having cleared the woods and created model farms of several acres — in contrast to the great artisan, feudal farms — the Cistercians built their great abbeys. The order's constructions reflected the austerity of its Rule. Neither towers nor porches were built; there was no sculpture and no stained glass windows. Whereas Cluniac churches were covered with gold and paintings, Cistercian churches were bare. Stones were left undressed.

'The Cathedral Builders' — Jean Gimpel, 1961

south aisle of the nave — 1150-60.

I say naught of the vast height of your churches, their immoderate length, their superfluous breadth, the costly polishings, the curious carvings and paintings which attract the worshipper's gaze and hinder his attention, and seem to me in some sort a revival of the ancient Jewish rites. Let this pass, however: say that this is done for God's honour. But I, as a monk, ask of my brother monks . . . 'Tell me, ye poor (if, indeed, ye be poor), what doeth this gold in your sanctuary?' And indeed the bishops have an excuse which monks have not; for we know that they, being debtors to the wise and the unwise, and unable to excite the devotion of carnal folk by spiritual things, do so by bodily adornments. But we [monks] who have now come forth from the people; we who have left all the precious and beautiful things of the world for Christ's sake; all things fair to see or soothing to hear, sweet to smell, delightful to taste, or pleasant to touch — in a word, all bodily delights — whose devotion, pray, do we monks intend to excite by these things? What profit, I say, do we expect therefrom? The admiration of fools, or the oblations of the simple? Or, since we are scattered among the nations, have we perchance learnt their works and do we yet serve their graven images? To speak plainly, doth the root of all this lie in covetousness, which is idolatry; and do we seek not [spiritual] profit, but a gift? If thou askest: 'How?' I answer, 'In a strange fashion.' For money is thus artfully scattered in order that it may multiply; it is expended that it may give increase, and the prodigality giveth birth to plenty; for at the very sight of these costly yet marvellous vanities men are more kindled to offer gifts than to pray. Thus wealth is drawn up by ropes of wealth, thus money bringeth money; for I know not how it is that, whatsoever more abundant wealth is seen, there do men offer more freely. These eyes are feasted with relics cased in gold, and their purse-strings are loosed. They are shown a most comely image of some saint, whom they think all the more saintly that he is the more gaudily painted. Men run to kiss him, and are invited to give; there is more admiration for his comeliness than veneration for his sanctity . . . The church is resplendent in her walls, beggarly in her poor; she clothes her stones in gold, and leaves her sons naked . . .

from the Apologia — St. Bernards defence
of the Cistercian attitude towards Cluniac
churches, written circa 1125.

The S. aisle and nave wall seen from the top of the stairway in the S. tra

There was nothing whatever new about Cîteaux. The monks simply wanted to return to the Rule of St. Benedict in all its simplicity. Far from being innovators, they were making it their chief concern to clean house and rid the Order of the many innovations that cramped the monastic life and made contemplation difficult or even impossible.

The first thing that shamed them was the realization that, in the course of centuries, monks had devised specious excuses for softening the Rule and making its burden on the flesh easier and easier. Some of these excuses were legitimate. When the Cluniacs asserted that monks in northern climates ought to be permitted to wear warmer clothing, they had been quite within their rights. St. Benedict explicitly allowed a certain freedom in the matter of clothing. However, the Cistercians seem to have felt that the use of fur coats and fur-lined jackets, and garments that were more or less ornamental, went beyond the legitimate interpretation of this rule. For their part, they would allow the monks to increase the *quantity* of their clothing in winter, without any substantial change in the *quality*. They could wear both their robes and both their cowls at the same time if they had to — but no furs. Less legitimate, however, was the interpretation of the Rule — which some Benedictine monks are supposed to have made — about abstinence from meat. St. Benedict had prohibited the flesh of four-footed animals. These casuists pointed out that chickens and ducks and quails and partridges and turkeys and pheasants had only two feet and therefore were not forbidden. Not everybody made use of this loophole, but the Cluniacs were notorious for their ingenuity in dressing up fish and vegetables and serving up spiced and seasoned dishes in quantities and varieties that made meat unnecessary. One of the chief concerns of the founders of Cîteaux was to return to St. Benedict's 'two portions' (*duo pulmentaria*), with black bread and a few extra fruits in season.

'The Waters of Siloe' — Thomas Merton, 1950

True, not all of Bernard's daughter houses enjoyed the same advantages. When his cousin, Godfrey de la Roche, founded Fontenay, he had to drain the swampy valley and collect its waters into many ponds before building his charming abbey — which was, according to the meaning written into its name, to 'swim upon fountains'. These valley monasteries developed within the Cistercian Order a beautiful spiritual symbolism by their names alone, eloquent and harmonious names full of poetry and simple mysticism, in which the image of 'waters' and 'fountains' and 'springs' plays a very important part. It was before St. Teresa of Avila wrote her famous allegory of contemplative prayer and the various *aguas* by which the soul is irrigated.

Steeped in the language and imagery of Scripture, the Cistercians were acutely alive to the spiritual and poetic possibilities of their surroundings, which they condensed into names like Fountains, Clairvaux ('Clear Valley', or 'Valley of Light'), Trois Fontaines ('Three Fountains'), Vauluisant ('Shining Valley'), Aiguebelle (*Aqua Bella,* 'Beautiful Water'), Senanque (*Sana Aqua,* 'Clean Water'), Clairmarais ('Clear Marsh'), Bonaigue (*Bona Aqua,* 'Good Water), Fontfroide ('Cold-Spring'), Mellifont ('Fount of Honey') —

'The Waters of Siloe' — Thomas Merton, 1950

A stream running to the Skell from West Applegarths: such streams provided the Abbey's supply of pure water.

The north doorway of the Chapel of the Nine Altars — 1220-50.

The arches leading into the chapter house — 1160-80

These vast edifices were miracles of construction. So were the non-monastic cathedrals served by secular canons, which the Normans raised in London, York, Old Sarum, Lichfield, Lincoln and Winchester; for the last a whole royal wood was felled. They were built without any but the most elementary mechanism for moving and lifting large weights, by men whose wealth consisted almost entirely of crops, flocks and herds and whose sole means of transport were wheeled carts drawn by oxen. To realise the magnitude of their achievement one has only to reckon what it would cost, even with modern machinery and power, to rebuild in stone every cathedral and parish church in England. Yet this is what the men of the twelfth and thirteenth centuries did at a time when the population was only a small fraction of its present size. 'It was as though,' a chronicler wrote, 'the very world had shaken herself and cast off her old age, and was clothing herself everywhere with a white robe of new churches.' Faith alone could have caused men to sacrifice and accomplish so much.

'The Story of England'
— Arthur Bryant, 1953

Something must now be said about that great system of filiation and visitation which went so far to make up what has been called the 'Cistercian idea.' Before the time of Stephen Harding, the Order existed only in germ, in a single convent, but under him, that convent grew into the head of a vast monastic confederacy, extending through every country in Europe. This is so well described by Newman, that I cannot refrain from quoting his own words. With the disorders of other monastic systems before his eyes, 'Stephen determined on instituting a system of reciprocal visitation between the abbeys of his Order. He might, as abbot of Citeaux, have constituted himself the head of this increasing congregation; but his object was not to lord it over God's heritage, but to establish between the Cistercian abbeys a lasting bond of love. The body of statutes which he presented to his brethren in the general chapter of 1119, was called the Chart of Charity. In its provisions, the whole Order is looked ujpon as one family, united by ties of blood; Citeaux is the common ancestor of the whole, and the first four abbeys founded from it, La Ferté, Pontigny, Clairvaux and Morimond, as its four eldest daughters, respectively governed the abbeys sprung from them. The abbot of Citeaux was called *Pater universalis ordinis*; he visited any monastery that he pleased, and wherever he went the abbot gave up his place to him. On the other hand, the abbots of the four filiations, as they were termed, visited Citeaux, besides which each abbot went every year to inspect the abbeys which had sprung from his own. Every year a general chapter was held at Citeaux, which all the abbots in the Order, except some whose houses were in very distant countries, were obliged to attend under heavy penalties. The chief abbot of each filiation could, with the advice of other abbots, depose any one of his subordinate abbots who after admonition continued to violate the Rule; and even the head of the whole Order might be deposed by the four abbots, though not without a general chapter, or in the case of urgent necessity, in an assembly of abbots of the filiation of Citeaux. Each abbey was to receive with joy any of the brethren of the other Cistercian abbeys, and to treat him as though he were at home. Thus the most perfect union was to be preserved amongst the whole body; and if any discord arose in the general chapter, the abbot of Citeaux might, with the help of other abbots, called in by himself, settle the question in dispute. This is but a faint outline of the famous Chart of Charity, which was copied by many others, and in part even by that of Cluny.'

The Yorkshire Archaeological and Topographical Journal, Vol. 10, 1886 — J. T. Fowler

The south-east corner of the cloister showing: doorways to chapter house and parlour, day-stairs to monks' dormitory (1160-80), linen cupboard, and entrance to warming house with muniment room above (1180-1210).

The lay-brothers' range, N. end (cellarium and parlour) 1160-80: the vaulting is circa 1180-90. This vaulted room with its 300ft. long vista, the largest in Europe, was originally divided into small rooms by cross walls.

In 1128 the first Cistercian house in England was founded at Waverley in Surrey. But it was among the desolate Yorkshire hills and the remote valleys of the Welsh Marshes that the Order made its chief settlements. It was part of its Rule that its monks should live far from the haunts of men, in silence and austerity, and support themselves by their own labour. Even their rough, homespun woollen tunics and cowls were undyed, giving them their name of white monks in contrast to the black monks of the older Rule. Their simplicity of life and love of solitude and country pursuits made a deep appeal to the English. By the end of Stephen's reign there were twenty Cistercian monasteries in Yorkshire alone, and forty in the kingdom. Fountains, founded in 1132 on waste ground in Skeldale by a dozen pioneers from St. Mary's, York, grew from a few huts under an elm tree into the great abbey of St. Mary's. Rievaulx, Jervaux, Byland and Kirkstall, Tintern, Valle Crucis, Neath, Abbey Dore and Margam, raised in the twelfth and rebuilt in the thirteenth and fourteenth centuries, were among the grandest achievements of the Middle Ages. Bare of ornament, sculpture and painting, their grave, simple outlines have still the power, even in ruin, to stir the heart after five centuries. Equally impressive were the woods the monks planted round their homes and the sheep-runs the lay brethren or *conversi* — drawn from the peasant class — made on the bleak northern and western hills. They were the most enlightened landlords and finest farmers of the age, sowing alternate corn and grass leys and transforming scrubby wilderness with flocks that grazed by day on the uplands and folded at night on the barley ploughlands. Theirs was an instinctive genius for blending the works of God and man; in the Great Coxwell barn in Berkshire we can still see the reverence and skill with which they turned nature to human ends while enriching and beautifying it. 'Laborare est orare', was their founder's motto: to work is to pray. They built roads and bridges, drained marshes and planted trees, quarried stone, wrought in wood and metal, laid out gardens and vineyards, and bred fine horses, cattle and sheep. To them England owed the noble Lion breed whose golden hoof raised the Cotswold towns and villages. They made her wool as famous as their brother monks of Cîteaux made the vineyards of the stony Côte d'Or. And if the great names of Chambertin and Clos de Vougeot still recall for lovers of wine the skill of the French Cistercians, their brethren in England are commemorated by the homely cheese which the monks of Jervaux made from ewe's milk in lonely Wensleydale.

The Story of England
Arthur Bryant, 1953

I. Inasmuch as we are known to be servants of the One True King, Lord and Master, albeit unprofitable, we therefore make no claim for worldly advantage of temporal gain on our abbots and brother monks, whom in divers places devotion to God shall call through us, the most wretched of men, to live under regular discipline. For, in our desire for their profit and that of all sons of holy Church, we are not disposed to lay any burden upon them or to effect anything calculated to diminish their substance, lest in striving to grow rich at their expense, we may not escape the sin of avarice, which is declared by the apostle to be servitude to idols.

II. Nevertheless we desire for love's sake to retain the cure of their souls, so that if they shall essay to swerve from their sacred purpose and the observance of the holy Rule — which God forbid — they may through our solicitude return to righteousness of life.

III. We will therefore and command them to observe the Rule of St. Benedict in all things as it is observed in the new monastery. Let the monks put no other interpretation upon the holy Rule but what the holy fathers, our predecessors, namely the monks of the new minster, have understood and maintained; and as we today understand and uphold it, so let them do also.

Excerpts from 'Carta Caritatis' (Charter of Love), the fundamental constitution of the Cistercians, written by an Englishman, Stephen Harding, second Abbot of Cîteaux, circa 1117. 'English Historical Documents II' — D. C. Douglas and A. W. Greenaway, 1959

Benedictine monks were bound by the three obligations of poverty, chastity, and obedience. The Cistercians gave a very severe meaning to the first of these. They described themselves as new soldiers of Christ, poor with the poor Christ — *novi milites Christi cum paupere Christo pauperes* — and lived up to their profession. They slept on straw, in their habit, and abstained not only from meat but largely from articles of food which other monks habitually used . . . To possess anything of one's own was a crime always ranked as equal to theft in the laws of the order.

The vow of obedience does not seem to have been kept with special severity, but great efforts were made to preserve the vow of chastity. No monk might speak to a woman alone. The porter was not even allowed to give alms to the poor women of the neighbourhood, save in times of famine, and then only at the express order of the abbot. Women were not allowed within the walls of the monasteries to work in kitchen or laundry. They were not even allowed in the neighbourhood of outlying farms, except when men could not be found to milk the cows, and then the milking had to be done outside the walls. Special care was exercised to keep women of notorious character at a considerable distance.

Women were admitted to the church for nine days at its dedication. This was the only occasion when women might enter, and so long as they were present, services were curtailed to the utmost extent. In 1192, women entered the monastery of Bellevaux on the feast of St. Peter. The general chapter put the abbot and monks on bread and water for a day and ordered each monk to have a private flogging. In 1205 the abbot of Pontigny allowed the Queen of France and her suite to enter his abbey, and spent two days in the infirmary. Though permission to enter had been given by the Pope and the abbot of Cîteaux, the general chapter considered the action of the abbot to have gone beyond the terms of this permission. He was not allowed to sit in his stall or to say mass for seven months, and was put for two days on bread and water.

A pamphlet, 'Fountains Abbey the monks and the buildings' — Rev. A. W. Oxford, 1921

The remains of the gatehouse (13th C.) near the present entrance to the Abbey.

One point in the Cistercian rule, which arose from this self-contained ideal and had an important influence upon the planning of Cistercian buildings, was the division of the brethren of each abbey into monks (*monachi*) and lay brothers (*conversi*). The Cistercian monk was a clerk who could read and write. Like a Benedictine monk, he was not necessarily a priest, although it became very general for monks to proceed to priest's orders. His duties lay in the church and cloister, and, unless he held an office such as that of cellarer or kitchener, he was not immediately concerned with the business affairs of his convent. These, which in Benedictine houses were largely transacted by tenants or hired labourers and servants, were performed in Cistercian houses by the *conversi*. A *conversus* was a layman who had turned from the service of the world to that of God. He entered the convent as a novice and in due course made his profession. He was precluded from learning to read or write and from taking holy orders. He was taught a few prayers and psalms by heart, but his business was manual labour in the convent workshops, or in its fields and granges. On ordinary work-days he had to attend part of the night-office and, if he was not stationed in a grange, had to come to compline. He observed the other hours by the recitation of special prayers at his work. His life was regulated by statutes which in respect of abstinence, silence and other similar essentials resembled those of the monks. The *conversi* had their own separate common rooms in the cloister buildings, their own quire in the church and their own infirmary. They rose at an hour which was specially calculated to allow them enough sleep before their day's work: their chapter was held by the abbot only on Sundays and certain feast-days. Thus the convent was provided with all the workmen whom it needed. Some *conversi* were deputed to live upon the convent granges, each of which had a *conversus* as prior. The white frocks and cowls of the monks gave the Cistercians their distinctive name of white monks as opposed to the Benedictines or black monks: the dress of the *conversus* was a cloak (*cappa*), tunic, stockings (*caligae*), boots (*pedules*) and a hood (*capucium*) covering only the shoulders and breast.

'English Monasteries' — A. Hamilton Thompson
1923

As the *conversi* far outnumbered the choir monks in the great days of Fountains, it would be interesting to know what sort of manual labour was allocated to the choir monks. Presumably they grew vegetables and herbs and flowers, and took care of the orchard and the dairy, the pets and the poultry, though butter and other delicacies were only allowed in the infirmaries and the guest house, and were therefore not needed on a large scale. The ground lying at the east end of the church was used as a burial place for the choir monks, and the land beyond it, now an extensive lawn, may have been the scene of the choir monks' labours. We do not know where the laybrothers were buried, but doubtless they were separate in death, as they had been in life, from the choir monks.

'The Fountains Story' — A. M. Wilkinson, 1957

The south face of the lay-brothers' reredorter — 1160-80.

Windows in the lay-brothers' dormitory, S. end: they are from 1180-1210 but made to match the earlier style of the N. end.

On places in which lay-brothers keep silence.

In those workshops where the monks keep silence, let them (lay-brothers) also keep it. Nor let them enter any one of them without permission. Moreover, let them keep silence completely in their dormitory and refectory, and in addition to this in all other places, unless perhaps they speak by order of the Abbot or Prior or also of the Cellarer, if this authority has been given to the Cellarer. Let shoemakers keep silence among themselves and with others, unless perhaps the Abbot has given them another location outside their workplace; there they speak amongst themselves in the presence of the master. The same applies to all artisans at the monastery, weavers, millers, tanners. Only smiths are allowed to speak where they work, since they could hardly keep silence in their work without detriment to their performance. Master masons, shoemakers or artisans of this sort may not speak with their men on the days when they do not work or during the evening hours when they have left their work. Similarly those in granges keep silence in oratory, dormitory, refectory and warming house, within boundaries set for this purpose. Elsewhere they may speak to their masters when the necessity arises. And it

The large corbel in the wall of the lay-brothers' reredorter at the intersection with their infirmary. (The groove in the wall indicates a pentise, or covered way.)

should be known that they are not allowed to speak without their hoods, unless while working or constrained by illness. Shepherds and cowherds may speak with their juniors and their juniors with them during work. Let them greet someone who greets them and, if a traveller should ask the way, tell him briefly. But if there is talk on other matters, they should answer that they may not speak. This should be their answer to anyone harassing them or urging them to speak; unless in pressing circumstances they have indulgence from their Abbot.

Cistercian Statutes circa 1256 — 'Yks. Arch. & Top. Journal', Vol. 10 1886

A lamp niche at the N. end of the dormitory by the night-stairs.

The north wall of the lay-brothers' infirmary, showing its one-time location on tunnels built over the Skell — 1180-1210.

The lay-brothers' range: cellarium or store-room (left) and refectory (right), with the cellarer's office mid-way; above is the dormitory extending the whole length. 13 bays to the N. have rounded windows (1160-80) and 9 bays to the S. have pointed ones (1180-1210).

The word cellarium is often used as a general term for the whole of the ground level of the lay-brothers' range, but it is here used in its specific sense of 'store rooms' (see glossary). Originally the 22 bays of the range were divided by walls into smaller rooms as follows (N. to S.): 2 bays, through-way into cloister; 6 bays, cellarium; 2 bays, cellarer's through-way or parlour; 12 bays, refectory.

(The original spelling is used in the following quotation):

The Fame of the sanctity of the cistercian Monks at Reival Abbey, (the first of that order in Yorkshire), having been extended to the benedictin Monastery of St. Mary at York, several of the Monks there, finding too great a relaxation in the observance of the rules, were desirous to withdraw themselves to follow the stricter rules observed by the Monks of Reival. But Galfrid their Abbot opposed their removal, as being a reflection upon his government of the Abbey; whereupon in A.D. 1132 (Henry I.) Richard, the Prior went to Thurstin, Archbishop of York, to desire he would visit the Abbey, and regulate what was amiss therein, and assist them in their design of withdrawing themselves. The day of visitation being come, the Archbishop attended by many grave and discreet Clergy, Canons, and other religious men went to St. Mary's Abbey, whither the Abbot had convoked several learned men, and a multitude of Monks from different parts of England, that by their aid he might oppose the Archbishop, if requisite, and correct the insolence of those brethren who wanted to leave the Abbey. On the 6th October, A.D. 1132, that Archbishop arrived at the Monastery when the Abbot with a multitude of Monks, opposed his entrance into the Chapter, with such a number of persons as attended him; whereupon an uproar ensued, and the Archbishop, after interdicting the Church and Monks, returned, and the Prior, Sub-prior, and eleven Monks withdrew themselves, and were joined by Robert a Monk of Whitby, who went along with them, and were maintained at the Archbishop's expence in his own house for eleven weeks and five days.

The Abbot sent his complaint against the Archbishop and those monks to the King, and at the same time to the Bishops, Abbots, and the neighbouring monasteries. On the other hand, Archbishop Thurstin, to prevent any ill consequences of those letters from the Abbot, wrote at large to William, Archbishop of Canterbury, the apostolic Legate, giving an ample account of the whole proceedings, and of the motives which had induced the Monks to have recourse to his protection, for withdrawing themselves from their Abbot and Monastery, where they thought they could no longer continue with a safe conscience, as not fulfilling the rules of their order.

The Abbot did not cease by messages to persuade the withdrawn monks to return to their Monastery, whilst they, at the Bishop's house spent most of their time in fasting and prayer. However two of them were prevailed upon to quit the rest, and go back, and yet one of the two repenting, soon returned to those who were for a more strict way of life.

At Christmas the Archbishop being at Ripon, assigned to the monks some land in the patrimony of St. Peter, about three miles west of that place, for erecting a Monastery. The spot of ground had never been inhabited unless by wild beasts, being overgrown with wood and brambles, lying between two steep hills and rocks, covered with wood on all sides, more proper for a retreat of wild beasts than the human species; this was called Skell-dale, that is the vale of Skel, a rivulet running through it from the west to the eastwards part of it: the Archbishop also gave to them a neighbouring village called Sutton. Richard, the Prior of St. Mary's at York, was chosen Abbot by the Monks, being the first of this Monastery of Fountains, with who they withdrew into this uncouth desert, without any house to shelter them in that winter season, or provisions to subsist on, but entirely depended on the divine providence. There stood a large elm in the midst of the vale, on which they put some thatch or straw, and under that they lay, eat, and prayed: the Bishop for a time supplying them with bread, and the rivulet with drink. Part of the day some spent in making wattles to erect a little Oratory, whilst others cleared some ground to make a little garden.

An ancient elm tree south of the Abbey.

On the south-side of the house where the Abbey stood, about the mid-way in ascending the hill, are 5 or 6 Yew trees, all yet 1757 growing (except the largest which was blown down a few years ago); they are of an almost incredible size, the circumference of the trunk of one of them is at least 14 feet, about a yard from the ground, and the branches in proportion to the trunk; they are nearly all of the same bulk; and are so nigh each other, as to make an excellent cover, almost equal to that of a thatched roof. Under these trees we are told by tradition, the Monks resided till they built the Monastery; which seems to me very probable, if we consider how little a Yew-tree increases in a year, and to what a bulk these are grown.

The two surviving yew trees of the seven known to have been in existence at the time of the founding of the Abbey.

The Winter being over, the Monks resolved to follow the rule of the cistercian order and accordingly they sent messengers to St. Bernard at Claraval, signifying what they had done, and their resolution of submitting themselves to his rule, acquainting him with their reasons for withdrawing from St. Mary's Abbey at York; the Archbishop likewise wrote to him on their behalf. This holy Abbot returned an answer to them commending their zeal and exhorting them to persevere. He wrote likewise to Archbishop Thurstin, extolling his charity towards those pious Persons; and to the Abbot of York, in answer to his complaints against those Monks who had withdrawn themselves.

With the messengers, who had been sent to Claraval, St. Bernard returned one Geoffrey, a Monk of this Monastery; who instructed those he had committed to his direction in the Cistercian rule, and caused them to build cottages for their cells and offices. Their number was likewise increased by ten Priests and Laymen, who resorted to them, and were received as novices; but their possessions were not yet enlarged, nor had they any other sustenance; but what the Archbishop allowed them; and that year proving scarce, they were reduced to such straits, that after the Abbot had been round the neighbourhood to beg without success, they were reduced to feed on the leaves of trees, and herbs gathered in the fields, and boiled with a little salt.

'An Ecclesiastical History of Yorkshire' — Dr. Burton, 1757

. . . and on a knoll, between the bridge and the mill, are the venerable yew-trees, which, beyond doubt, have witnessed all the changes of Fountain Dale from a period long before the Conquest. They are still known as the 'Seven Sisters', although but 2 now remain. These are of great size, with twisted, fast-decaying trunks, one of which is 25 ft. in circumference. De Candolle supposed these trees to be more than 12 centuries old; but they may very well be far more ancient, since it is impossible to ascertain at what time their growth ceased. They are at any rate the most certain relics which the valley now contains, of the first two years during which the fugitives from St. Mary's led their struggling life here.

Murray's 'Handbook for Travellers in Yorkshire', 1882

The Skell in flood, passing the privy of the west guest hou[se], the river acted as a natural discharger of waste.

The undercroft of the monks' dormitory, N. end, parts of which are pre the fire of 1147. The piers belong to the later 12th C. remodelling. The exact function of this room is not known.

The Fountains Chronicle, (*Narratio de fondatione Fontanis Monasterii*) written in simple monkish Latin, is one of the most fascinating documents in English monastic history, because it contains an eye-witness account of the adventures of the first generation of monks. This Chronicle was dictated by a very old monk called Serlo to a young monk called Hugh at Kirkstall Abbey about the year 1207. Serlo's own words are the credentials with which Hugh introduces his subject. 'It is now the 69th year of my profession, and when I entered Fountains I was beginning my 30th year. When the monks left the monastery at York I myself was present. I had known their names and faces from my boyhood, I was brought up among them, and several of them were my relations. And although I am now far advanced in years, my memory remains unimpaired, and particularly retentive of what happened when I was young.'

Serlo became a monk at Fountains in 1138, and nine years later he was a member of the colony who were sent to found a daughter house at Barnoldswick. He later moved with the rest of that community to Kirkstall, where he spent the remaining years of his long life.

As Kirkstall was a daughter house of Fountains, the two monasteries were in constant touch with one another, and Kirkstall was officially visited at least once a year by the Abbot of her mother house, or his representative. It was the able and discriminating Abbot John of Fountains who invited Hugh and Serlo to write an account of the history of Fountains from her foundation in 1132 to the death of Abbot Ralph Haget in 1203. No doubt old Serlo, and his reminiscences, were only too well known to his contemporaries, but the far-sighted Abbot John recognised the value of preserving them for posterity. Hugh was probably the most literary member of the community at Kirkstall, and his intimacy with Ralph Haget had kept him in contact with the Fountains community.

Hugh included in his chronicle six letters which had a bearing on the Fountains story, a long and important letter from Thurstan to Archbishop Corbeil of Canterbury,* and five short letters from Bernard.

'The Fountains Story' — A. M. Wilkinson, 1957

* see next column

'For when strife, dissension, and abuse arise among the brethren, and altercations and murmurings against those in authority, it is clear from what kind of a root such evil sprang. How then can we be so mad as to call ourselves monks of the blessed Benedict, who forbids with many threats all those things which we in our great presumption are not afraid to do. For these are his own words — "Scandal, and idle talk and jokes we ban everywhere and absolutely; we will not permit a disciple to open his mouth to say such things." And elsewhere he says, "At all times monks ought to aim at silence, but especially in the night hours." How diligently this decree is observed, every one knows who has had an opportunity of seeing our habits. For while some of us go into the church after collation; others wander away for trifling and useless chatter, as if the malice of the day were not sufficient unless that of the night were also added. And why recall our extravagance in diet? For many dishes are added over and above what was ordered by the blessed Benedict, giving the wicked impression that the rule is best observed where the greatest superfluity can be enjoyed. Why should I speak of our exquisite delicacies, our variously flavoured sauces, our many dainties? Assuredly new stimulation is applied to the full and over-gorged belly, so that, while there is hardly a scrap of room left in it, the voluptuous desire of eating still grows. And though the burdened lungs belch forth intolerable stinks, a new variety of food removes satiety. The same is true of the agreeable and splendid variety of drinks, of the elaborate delicacy of raiment. These were not the sentiments or the teachings of our blessed Benedict, according to whose rule we make our profession. For the rule looks at warmth, not colour in dress; it seeks not savour in the articles of food, but satisfies necessity with a frugal diet. For no other reason was the rich man in the gospel condemned than because he wore costly raiment and fared sumptuously every day, and because he employed profitable things unprofitably, and wearied himself with superfluity, whereas he might with them have supplied the wants of many of the poor. But if there be any failure in observing the established rule, how wretched shall the transgressor be when he shall stand in their assembly. Assuredly, if I mistake not, he falls among those of whom the Psalmist saith, "Verily they shall be dispersed to their eating, and if they are not satisfied they will murmur." Now let us gather together these ill-natured frivolities, this vain and harmful gossip, these luxurious feastings, these frequent and splendid potations, the other countless superfluities, and I think we shall make a foul and noisome heap. If I mistake not, chastity is with difficulty preserved in such surroundings.'

'The Fountains Chronicle' — Hugh of Kirkstall, 1207. (This excerpt is the exhortation for stricter observance of the rule of Prior Richard — later to be first abbot of Fountains — to his abbot at St. Mary's Abbey of York, in 1132: it is contained in a letter from Archbishop Thurstan of York to the Archbishop of Canterbury, quoted by Hugh in the Chronicle).

ON THE ELM

There was an elm in the middle of the valley, leafy as this type of tree is, which for the animals lying beneath it tempers the cold in winter and in summer the heat with the kindliness of its leaves. Here the holy men gathered to seek shelter in its shade. The tree stood in the centre and they lay around it, keeping off the harsh winter as best they could with straw and grasses thrown over them. Still the elm remains unharmed, green with its leaves and thick foliage, as proof to posterity of the humble state in which our mother, the church of Fountains, was first founded. No cut timbers, no dressed stones, but a poor hovel and a kind of shepherd's hut, with humble turf as its roof. It is something well worth recording, the sight of the soldiers of Christ at the time of their recruitment, conducting themselves loyally, living out the winter in tents. They all slept under the one tree, all sat at meals under the one tree, a poor convent but strong in the Lord; twelve priests and a deacon. The holy bishop served their bread, the stream flowing nearby their drink. At night they usually rose for vigils, sung psalms according to the rule, paid earnest attention to the prayer and summoned themselves to divine praise by mutual encouragement. By day they girded themselves for work, some weaving mats, others taking withies from the nearby wood to build an oratory; others, more prudent, set themselves to cultivating gardens. Nor was there time to break idle bread, nor to indulge in relaxation unless exhausted with work. Hungry they came to the table, tired to bed, never filled, but without a murmur. There was no sign of sadness to see there and no sound of complaint to hear, but with all wholeheartedness they blessed the Lord, poor in possessions but strong in faith.

'The Fountains Chronicle' — Hugh of Kirkstall, 1207

Frozen rushes near the site of the misericord.

THE MONK OF CLAIRVAUX WHOM SAINT BERNARD SENT TO THE MONASTERY OF FOUNTAINS

When all this had been accomplished, the messengers who had been sent to Clairvaux returned with letters from the holy abbot. They had in their company a certain monk from the monastery of Clairvaux called Geoffrey, a holy and religious man. There can be no doubt of the perfection of one who was so greatly valued by the blessed Bernard, and sent from his side to our fathers to establish them in the first principles of the order, the manner of life, and mode of conduct, according to the discipline of the order. I saw the man when I was still in my secular habit. He was of a great age and a modest gravity, a man strenuous in matters human and divine.

This Geoffrey, as we have said, came to Fountains, and was received by the brothers with reverence and fit honour. All were comforted at his arrival, and when they heard the message of the holy abbot, they bowed their necks to the Cistercian yoke, hearing the word from the lips of the old man and keeping it. According to his counsel they built huts, established workshops, singing and chanting as he taught them. They received with reverence the holy message, and, as heated wax takes the impression of the seal, so they took the form of the holy institution. The man of Burgundy marvelled to find in Englishmen such frugality, such swift obedience, such abstinence in diet, such gravity of manners. He found them 'strong in faith, rooted in charity, patient in hope, most long-suffering in poverty'. Meanwhile the number of the brethren increased. Seven clerics and ten laymen joined them and were received as novices according to the discipline of the order.

The Abbey with a bakehouse oven in the foreground. (See the Introduction for the recent re-naming of this site as the 'northern industrial building'.)

ON HUNGER

And it happened, after some days, that hunger grew strong in our area and the holy men were severely pressed. There were no loaves to eat, no money to buy them, no harvest in the granaries, and a considerable mass of poor people flowed in their direction. The abbot went around the places nearby asking food for the brothers, and there was no-one to give it to them nor did anyone have the means to provide it. There was privation everywhere [and they were uncertain what to do]. To stay in one place was grim enough; to stay there lonely and without food completely impossible. Driven at last to the extremes of poverty, they stripped the leaves from the trees, gathered simple country herbs and, adding a little salt, cooked rations for the sons of the prophets. The elm under which they had long stayed benefitted them twice over: shelter in winter, food in summer. In this way they fed themselves, the holy men once used to luxuries, eating bread by weight and food by the measure; and bitter food at that. 'Death in a pot' it was, but the flour of faith added to it somewhat alleviated the unpleasantness of the cooking. These were our fathers who, while in deep poverty, planted our vine, and with the sweat of their brows granted to us the abundance which we have today. Considering that they lived for tomorrow, not for themselves, they weighed all that shortage of worldly things against the comfort of their descendents yet to be born. A certain proof was made for the future, of the greatness in God's eyes of the virtues of holy poverty, which has deserved its exalted place.

'The Fountains Chronicle' — Hugh of Kirkstall, 1207

The east face of the Abbey on a winter's day.

Trees in March, Kitchen Bank.

St. Alberic and his fervent community (Cîteaux 1098), performed the dedication of their monastery to God, under the special patronage and protection of the Blessed Virgin; and drew up a permanent rule to the following effect: 'Since the illustrious life, the exalted dignity, and the admirable sanctity of Blessed Mary, the glorious Mother of God, enlighten, direct, and instruct the whole Church of God; all the churches of our monasteries shall be henceforth founded and dedicated in her honour'. John, Abbot of Cîteaux, in his 'Liber Privilegiorum', remarks: 'This was the first Order in the Western Church dedicated in honour of the Blessed Virgin Mary.'

The circumstance that she was chosen to be the peculiar saint of the rising order, is in itself characteristic. One would have thought that the austerity of Alberic and Stephen would have led them to choose some martyr or some unbending confessor of the faith; but they rather raised their minds to her on whom the mind cannot rest without joy . . . She was the spotless lily of the valley, in which the King of Heaven deigned to take up His abode.

'A Concise History of the Cistercian Order' — a Cistercian monk, 1852

But the first two years were a lean time for the monks at Fountains, and even their stout-hearted Abbot began to wonder whether there was any prospect of making good in Skelldale. So, after much heart-searching, in the late summer of 1134, when Richard went out to Cîteaux for the General Chapter, he asked Bernard to find them another site in France. Bernard agreed, and a new site in the diocese of Langres was actually chosen and offered. But when Richard returned home, he found the situation transformed. Hugh, Dean of York, who was now old and ailing, had decided that it was time for him to 'make his soul', so he came to Fountains, bringing with him a large fortune and a fine library of books.

The early Cistercians, in obedience to the principles of their Order, refused to become rentiers, they could accept land, and money, but not draw rents. According to Cistercian custom Dean Hugh's fortune must be divided into three parts, for the poor, for the fabric and for general monastic purposes.

It must have been soon after the arrival of Hugh that Thurstan's Foundation Charter was granted to the Fountains monks, as the first witness is Hugh's successor Dean William of York.

'The Fountains Story' — A. M. Wilkinson, 1957

TURSTAN, by the grace of God Archbishop of York, to the Archbishop of Canterbury, and to all Bishops, Abbats, Clerks, Barons, and Laymen of all England, and to their successors, greeting. We make known to you all, that we have given in alms to God and St. Mary of Fountains, and to the Abbat and Monks, part of the Wood of Herleshow, according to the boundary which we have pointed out to Richard, the first Abbat of the same place; and that we have allowed (or conceded) that portion of land which Wallef, son of Archil, our vassal, gave to the same church, which is adjoining the same wood in which we have founded the said church. Moreover we have given to the aforesaid church, two carucates of land, in wood and open ground in Sutton, except one ploughland, which lies on the east side of the way leading from Ripon to Stainley; and let this be clear to you all, forasmuch as they have professed to live according to the rule of the Blessed Benedict. All the aforesaid things we have granted in alms aforesaid; quit and free of all land-service due to us and our successors, under these witnesses:- Witness, William the Dean, and William the Treasurer, Hugh the Precentor, Osbert the Archdeacon, Walter the Archdeacon, Fulk the Canon, Serlo the Canon, William de Percy, Anfrid the Canon, Garfrid the Canon, Achard the Canon, Letold the Canon, and all the Canons of St. Peter. Witnesses also, William Marton, and Robert de Pinkney, and Simon, and Clibert, and Gislebert, Canons of St. Wilfrid. Witness also, William the Steward, and Robert the Constable, and William Unahait, and Richard the Thief-taker, and Hugh son of Hulric, and Robert of Herleshow, and Wallief of Studley, and Richard his brother, and Hulchil the Bailiff.

The charter of Archbishop Thurstan, legally conveying land to the monks in 1134: 'Guide to Ripon and Fountains Abbey' — J. R. Walbran, 1844

The Skell emerging from the tunnels under the infirmary (1220-50).

The abbey mill* is a long three-storied building, measuring 23½ feet in width internally. It was originally at least 100 feet in length, but the north end has been destroyed and a modern structure of smaller dimensions than the old work built on its site.

Unlike the other buildings that have been described, the mill retains its roof and floors, and is still in working order; the northern half being used as of old as a corn mill, and the southern end as the saw mill of the Studley Royal estate. Originally there was but one wheel, in the centre of the building, but since the Suppression another has been added outside on the south-west.

The mill is mostly of the thirteenth century, but on the east side there remain parts of a structure anterior to the fire of 1147, with some later alterations.

Fountains Abbey — St. John Hope: 'Yorks.
Arch. Journal', Vol. 15 1898

* Not open to the public, but in time to be restored.

The abbey mill, 12th and 13th centuries.

When the news of Abbot Richard's death reached Fountains in the summer of 1139, and her monks had paid their tribute of praise and gratitude and grief for their noble founder, they despatched messengers to the Abbot of Clairvaux to obtain his consent for their choice of Richard the Prior as their second Abbot.

The Carta Caritatis laid down that the abbot of the mother house should preside when one of her daughters was electing a new abbot. All the monks, including the conversi, were to be present, and also the abbots of her daughter houses; and the new abbot was supposed to be chosen from the family. In this case Bernard could not be present, and he never, in fact, visited his English daughter houses, but he had to be consulted, though the election of Richard the Prior appears to have been a foregone conclusion. We must picture an assembly (when Bernard's consent had been obtained) consisting of all the Fountains choir monks and conversi, and also of the abbots of Newminster, Kirkstead and Louth Park, the three young daughter houses. William of Rievaulx, too, would almost certainly be there. It would be a sad and also happy occasion, and the Rule of silence must have been relaxed a little at the meeting of so many old friends. This second Richard had been sacristan at St. Mary's Abbey, and, according to Serlo, he was the original founder of the rebel group.

Serlo's world was small, and mostly bounded by the walls of the two monasteries he knew so well; as a result his chronicle has many omissions. For example he scarcely mentions the long and recurring journeys that were the lot of every conscientious Cistercian abbot. The second Richard, who longed only to pursue his devotions and fulfil his pastoral responsibilities at Fountains, had an obligation to visit three daughter houses every year, all lying more than 100 miles away, as well as to attend the General Chapter at Cîteaux and also visit Clairvaux; and we learn from another contemporary source that he travelled out to Rome with William of Rievaulx early in 1143 (the year of his Whitsuntide return to Fountains and also of his death) to oppose the election of William Fitzherbert as Archbishop Thurstan's successor. It is surprising to find the diffident Richard engaged in a public controversy of this kind . . . In view of these many extra-mural commitments, it is easy to understand why Abbot Richard II longed to escape from the high office of Abbot of Fountains.

'The Fountains Story' — A. M. Wilkinson, 1957

View looking north over the E. end of the remains of the monks' reredorter with its drain in the foreground. Behind are the three prison cells (left) and cellar (centre of picture). The abbot's house was over this site from the 14th C. onwards.

The Chapel of the Nine Altars: silhouetted forms of the 13th and 15th centuries.

Of Ralph Haget (Abbot of Fountains 1191-1203) however, who came next, we have more information, due not to Serlo, but to the redactor of his narrative, Hugh of Kirkstall, who had received the religious habit at the hands of this abbot and to whom Serlo appealed at this point. Ralph was the son of a well-known landed family in Yorkshire, and followed the ordinary career of a knight till his thirtieth year. Then, dissatisfied with the life he was living, he had recourse repeatedly for guidance to a lay brother of Fountains named Sunnulph, a man of unusual holiness of life. Sunnulph promised his prayers: 'Do you pray also,' he said, 'and let not your deeds hinder our common prayers.' Like Ailred before him, Ralph found it hard to break with the past. At last, rising one morning early in the dawn, with the spiritual crisis of his life upon him, he entered a neighbouring chapel and standing before the crucifix besought God to direct his path into the way of eternal life. He heard a voice from the figure on the Cross: 'And why comest thou not? Wherefore delayest thou so long?' Falling to the ground he replied with all his heart: 'Behold, Lord, behold, I come!' When day broke he made his way to Sunnulph, told him what had occurred, and promised to follow his advice. The old man was silent for a few moments, then replied: 'At Fountains shalt thou take the religious habit, and there, when thy race is run, shalt thou die.'

'The Monastic Orders in England' — D. Knowles, 1940

ON A REVELATION OF THE TRINITY

I shall tell of an event of which I often heard him speak himself, but which I mention with some trepidation, though I think it would be pointless to suppress it. One Sunday, when the holy convent was proceeding with Lauds, the psalm being sung at that moment was 'Confess to the Lord'. As the man of God concentrated his mind on the psalm, the hand of God appeared over him, and he saw a great vision, a glorious vision, the very Trinity itself appearing in three persons. I repeatedly asked of him in what shape and form this revelation appeared, but he said 'There was no shape there, nothing outlined, and yet I saw in a blessed vision three Persons in One. I saw', he said, 'and knew, the Father born of nothing, the Son born of one and the Holy Spirit proceeding from both. And the vision lasted until two verses of the aforementioned psalm were completely finished. From that hour and from then on, nothing has happened to me so sad, nothing ever of such trial that it is not tempered by the memory of this joyful vision. This is my memory, a solace during pain and a support in adversity; my delight and a jubilation in my heart, vigour for my faith and strength for my hope. Lastly, I am filled by the revelation with so much trust in my hope, that after this I have never been able to doubt my salvation, when the revelation of such a joyous vision has been made to me.' This the holy master sometimes told me of himself, and wept.

Abbot Ralph Haget's vision: 'The Fountains Chronicle' — Hugh of Kirkstall, 1207

Life of Blessed John

ABBOT OF FOUNTAINS (1203-1211)

The Abbot John was a native of York, of rich and powerful family. He had been already Abbot of Parcolude,* an Abbey founded from Fountains in the year of grace 1139.

His great liberality towards the poor caused him to be accused of seeking after a Bishopric, by seeking to gain the affection of the people, and by being well thought of by the great ones of the earth. He paid no attention one way or other to these speeches, but continued his good deeds as aforetime.

King John, yielding to the counsel of the wicked men of his court, was very severe upon the Cistercian Monasteries. He was so violent in his exactions, that the poor Monks were forced to sell their sacred vessels and priestly vestments, and even had to go out of their Monasteries, some to seek refuge in those of other Orders, others to find a subsistence where they could in the towns, and amongst the soldiers, or any where they could find it. Upon the Abbey of Fountains he imposed a tax of twelve hundred marks of silver, to be promptly paid.

The Abbot John, in this extremity, desiring to oblige the Almighty God to come and help him, opened his granaries and distributed all his provisions to those who were oppressed by the king, reserving nothing for his own wants. He was not deceived of his hope, for, during the whole time of this storm and tempest, his granaries failed not, and there was plenty for the poor. The Monks' habits also did not grow old or worn. At this time the number of Brethren so increased, that the Blessed John began to build a larger Church, which was not finished in his own days.†

In A.D. 1204, when the Blessed Abbot John, with some other Abbots of his Order, assembled together before King John, for to try and appease his anger, the King in great wrath commanded them to be thrown down beneath his horse's feet, that he might tread them underfoot. No one was found who would dare to execute this wicked command. The following night the King had a vision in his sleep, in which it appeared to him that he was made to stand in judgement before the Abbots of the Order of Cîteaux, and, being condemned, received a severe scourging on his back, with rods and whips, and for surety of the truth of what had taken place, he still felt the pain of it upon awaking. He told this to a certain Priest in his court, who counselled him to demand pardon of the Abbots for what he had done, saying that God had been very merciful to him in not punishing him more severely.

The King sent for the Abbots, who were all in great fear, expecting some fresh cruelty. They were astonished when they heard why they had been sent for, and gave God many thanks for that He had taken up their case.

'The Cistercian Fathers — Lives and Legends': trans. Henry Collins, Dublin, 1874

* Louth Park, Lincolnshire.
† The presbytery, finished by John II and John of Kent. Historical truth is confirmed up to this point in Hugh of Kirkstall's 'Fountains Chronicle'.

Presbytery walls, 1210-20: behind is Abbot Huby's tower, 1495-1526.

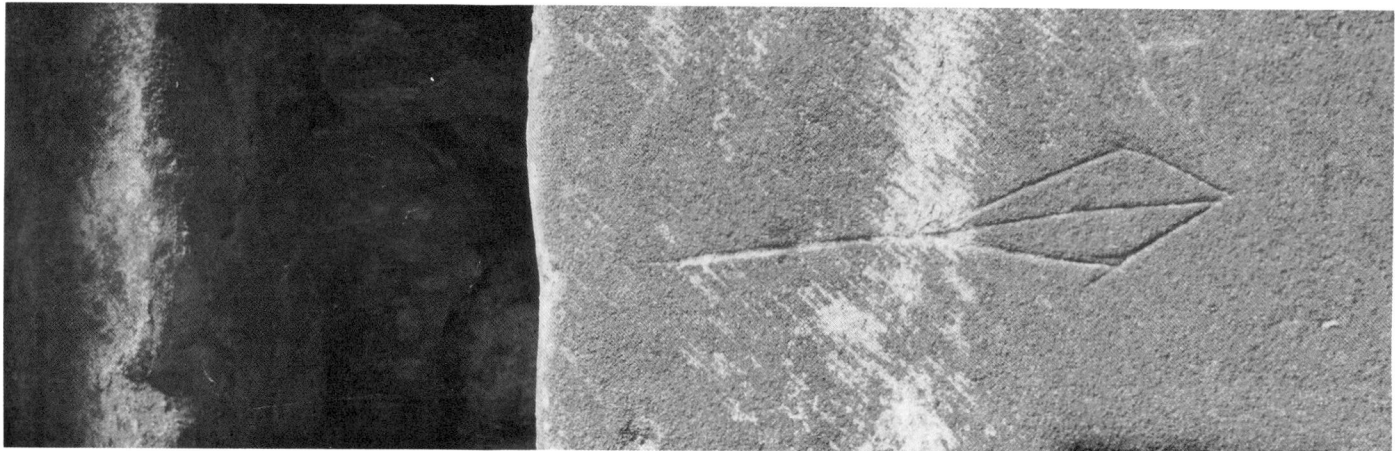

Above: a mason's mark, approximately half size, in the passage between the S. transept and the chapter house. Below: some of the original plaster on the walls of the day-stairs to the monks' dormitory. The plain grey-white surface is patterned in white without reference to the line of the stones underneath.

Mr T. W. Thornton, President of the Leeds Photographic Society, lectured last night at York to the Yorkshire Philosophical Society on the story of Fountains Abbey . . .

By whom, he asked, were these churches and monasteries built? Some averred that they were built by travelling parties of free masons, others said by free masons but not as the word is understood today. Some said the men who built them came from Como in Italy and were greatly skilled in their work. Whatever other gifts these men had they must have possessed the gift of concealing their footsteps, for there was not one word in the records that could be twisted into meaning this. But there were plenty of records of men who came together haphazard and were organised in order to do certain work. They (the skilled workers) left plenty of masons' marks behind them, marks which were connected with some of the oldest religions in the world, the mysteries of which we knew so little. There were some of these signs in York Minster. Was it possible that the same men worked in York and at Fountains Abbey and on the continent as well? If these men put their marks upon the work so that they should be payed for it, then, he pointed out, there were only nine masons' marks in Kirkstall . . . They (the churches and monasteries) must have been conceived by some master minds, but all traces of individuality had disappeared.

Speaking of the remarkable plaster used in the building (Fountains Abbey) Mr. Thornton explained that the plaster existed today, whilst the walls had crumbled and perished. It was a wonderful plaster, the manufacture of which was unknown to the present day. The plaster was impervious to fire. A photograph thrown on the screen demonstrated that whereas stonework had rotted away the plaster was still as good as the day upon which it was put in.

Report in the 'Yorkshire Herald', Nov 11th 1909

When Walter of Hereford sent laborers to the quarry at Vale Royal, he had his carpenters build one lodge of fourteen hundred boards to accommodate the stonecutters. The following year he built a smaller lodge of one thousand boards. Whether the stonecutters were paid by the piece or by the week, their lives centered in or around the lodge. In the morning they went to get their tools, they had lunch there, and in very hot weather they took siestas there. There were always one or more lodges at the workshop, and they can be seen located at the foot of buildings under construction in manuscript illuminations.

The lodges not only gave workers a place in which to eat and rest, but they provided a place in which stonecutters could work in bad weather. For this reason these lodges were very important during the winter months. Stonecutters stayed in the lodges then and, sheltered from the elements, prepared work for the masons who would return to the shop only with the coming of good weather. Yet nights were not spent in the lodges. In the cathedral cities, workers were housed in inns or in private homes. Due to the isolation of abbeys, wood dormitories were erected for workers engaged in monastic construction programs.

The lodge became, in addition to being a place for work and rest, a place in which problems of interest to all could be discussed. In a way it was a club, and this was the early beginning of masonic lodges in the modern sense.

'The Cathedral Builders' — Jean Gimpel, 1961

The 12th century N. aisle, with a window replaced in the 15th C.

The spiral staircase in the Chapel of the Nine Altars, leading to a wall passage and the roof, 1220-50.

The exterior of the S. transept chapels: the N. chapel (left) is 1150-60; the S. chapel (right) has a 15th C. extension, probably used as a sacristy.

Porters, cementers, and stonecutters were only one part of the family of stoneworkers; plasterers, plaster mixers, and masons made up the other part. The statutes of Étienne Boileau confirm this: 'The cementer and the plasterer are of the same status and the same lodge of masons in all respects.' The mason was above all else a stone layer. The English word explains this act of placing or setting stones, calling it 'setting' or 'laying'. The English words that designate various specialized workers are quite interesting since they reveal the origin of the word 'freemason' and give an insight into how 'operative' freemasonry (which preceded the contemporary 'speculative' freemasonry — composed of men not masons by profession: a social fraternal organization) was born and developed.

The Latin terms that designated workers who cut stone in the Middle Ages do not generally permit a distinction to be made between those who simply quarried the stone and those who cut the vault stones, window tracery, and monumental portal sculpture. The sculptors were lost among the general mass of stonecutters. This is really rather extraordinary to us, because an enormous difference seems to exist between those who perform a seemingly mechanical task, such as cutting blocks of stone, and those who sculpt, *with their soul*, the magnificent statues in the cathedrals. The truth is that for the great majority of men in the Middle Ages there was between a good *work* and a *masterpiece* only a difference of degree, not a difference of kind. The idea that there is an unbridgeable gulf between a worker and an artist (in the modern sense of the word) did not really occur until the Renaissance when it was expressed by intellectuals who judged, classified, and evaluated manual labor which was very foreign to them.

'The Cathedral Builders' — Jean Gimpel, 1961

N.B. As with most buildings of its kind and period in this country, there are no records dealing with the identity, hiring or payment of the skilled masons who built Fountains Abbey (ed.)

The S. wall of the nave: in the foreground are capitals of the chapter house doorway.

After terce on ordinary days, or the morning Mass when it was sung, the chapter was held, the abbot, or in his absence some other officer, presiding. The chapter began with the reading of the martyrology for the day, followed by a short office of prayer for the faithful departed, and then a portion of the rule of St. Benedict was read. This was the *chapter* the reading of which gave the name to the assembly. The names of those monks to whom different duties were assigned were written on a tablet, and were read out each week in chapter when all were present; and if a man knew of any hindrance to his performing what was set down to him, it was his duty to state it then and there, and to ask to be excused. If this were not done, and exemption had to be sought afterwards, it was regarded as a fault, for which pardon must be asked. After the reading of the tablet, a formal commemoration of all deceased members and associates (*familiares*) of the order was made, and on feast days, an instruction or sermon, according to the time, was delivered by the president or by some other appointed by him. This ended, the president said *Let us now speak of our order*, and commemoration was made by name of those recently dead, and the chanter read any letters which might have been received announcing deaths in other monasteries.

Then followed a specially monastic feature of the chapter — the public confession and punishment of faults. Any monk who knew that he had offended was formally to 'seek pardon' and state what he had done amiss. And if any knew of fault in another, he was to say so plainly in few words. The accused might deny the accusation if he felt it to be unjust, and the accuser was not to repeat it unless ordered to do so, but others who knew anything of the matter might speak. A rule which must have been very useful if strictly enforced, forbad a man who had been denounced to denounce his denouncer at the same chapter.

Cases which ordinarily came before the chapter and were dealt with there, were punished by penances such as loss of precedence in the convent, fasting on bread and water, and sometimes flogging, which was administered on the spot. Excommunication was used sometimes, and serious crimes were punished by imprisonment, exile, or expulsion from the order.

Whatever passed in chapter was to be kept secret, and was not even to be spoken of in any other place.

The Cistercian Order — an article by J. T. Micklethwaite: 'Yorkshire Archaeological Journal', Vol.15 1900

List of Abbotts and Place of Burial

1	Richard I	1132-1139	Rome
2	Richard II	1139-1143	Clairvaux
3	Henry Murdach	1144-1147	York Cathedral
	Maurice (1147-1148)		Rievaulx
	Thorold (1148-1150)		Trois Fontaines
4	Richard III	1150-1170	Chapter house, Fountains
5	Robert of Pipewell	1170-1180	Chapter house, Fountains
6	William of Newminster	1180-1190	Chapter house, Fountains
7	Ralph Haget of Kirkstall	1190-1203	Chapter house, Fountains
8	John of York	1203-1211	Chapter house, Fountains
9	John of Hessle	1211-1220	Ely Cathedral
10	John of Kent	1220-1247	Chapter house, Fountains
11	Stephen of Eston	1247-1252	Chapter house, Vaudey
12	William of Allerton	1253-1258	Chapter house, Fountains
13	Adam	1258-1259	Chapter house, Fountains
14	Alexander	1259-1265	Chapter house, Fountains
15	Reginald	1265-1274	Chapter house, Fountains
	Peter Alyng	(1274-1279)	Chapter house, Fountains
16	Nicholas	1279	Chapter house, Fountains
17	Adam	1280-1284	Chapter house, Fountains
	Henry Otley	(1284-1289)	Chapter house, Fountains
	Robert Thornton	(1289-1290)	Chapter house, Fountains
18	Richard Bishopton	1290-1311	Chapter house, Fountains
19	Richard Rigton	1311-1316	Chapter house, Fountains
20	Walter Coxwold	1316-1336	Chapter house, Fountains
21	Robert Copgrove	1336-1346	Chapter house, Fountains
22	Robert Monkton	1346-1369	The Church, Fountains
23	William Gower	1369-1384	Chapel of Nine Altars, F.
24	Robert Burley	1384-1410	The choir, Fountains
	Roger Frank	(1410-1413)	
25	John Ripon	1414-1435	Nave of church, Fountains
26	Thomas Paslew	1435-1442	Nave of church, Fountains
27	John Martin	1442	Nave of church, Fountains
28	John Greenwell	1442-1471	
29	Thomas Swinton	1471-1478	
30	John Darnton	1479-1495	
31	Marmaduke Huby	1495-1526	
32	William Thirsk	1526-1536	
33	Marmaduke Bradley	1536-1539	

N.B. Though there were 39 abbots of Fountains, six were not ascribed a number by the monastery, having been judged to have ruled unsatisfactorily. No indication of place of burial denotes lack of evidence, but it may be assumed to be in the church.

Corbels, 1160-80: left, in the chapter house; right, in the parlour.

The *Chapter-house* is E. Eng., but of an earlier character than the choir, and was possibly, as Mr Walbran suggests, the work of Abbot Richard Fastolph (1150-1170), who had been prior of Clairvaux, and may have brought the design from that great abbey. It is rectangular, and was divided into 3 aisles by a double row of 5 columns, the bases of which alone remain. This aisled Chapter-house is peculiar. It occurs at Jervaulx and at Beaulieu in Hampshire (both Cistercian), and at Netley (Benedictine) and Tintern (Cistercian). It is found only in monastic churches.

The brackets here are noticeable. The simple long leaf, ribbed in the middle, like the leaf of a hart's tongue fern, runs through the ornamentation of the abbey. Here two leaves are sometimes laid one on another. The abbots of Fountains, from 1170 to 1345, were (with two exceptions) buried here, and the coffins and tomb-slabs of 10 abbots (including the most northerly in the 2nd row from the east, that of John of Kent, the builder of the 9 altars) remain on the floor.

Murray's 'Handbook for Travellers in Yorkshire', 1882

The chapter house: the grave covers of the early abbots and three-tiered stone platforms once supporting benches.

LANDS ACQUIRED BY THE ABBEY OF FOUNTAINS DURING THE 12th CENTURY

Herbert de Arches gave lands in Bordley and Coniston in Craven.

Thurstin de Arches gave lands in Arncliffe and Kilnsey, and pasturage in Bordley.

Ernald, son of Beute, Ralph, Thomas and William his sons; and Michael son of William, gave lands in Dromonby, near Stokesley.

Nicholas de Braythwath, gave lands in Braithwaite, in Allerdale, Cumberland.

Philip de Braythwayth, and Jocelinus his son, gave lands in Braithwaite, near Kirkby Malzeard.

Reginald, the Clerk de Burnebusk, gave a messuage in Cockermouth, and lands, &c., in Crosthwaite in Allerdale, Cumberland.

Walter de Busce, Edith his wife, and William their son, gave lands and minerals in Kirk Heaton.

Nicholas de Caiton, gave lands in Ingerthorpe, Ripley, Ripon and Markenfield.

Alan de Calton and Hugh de Calton gave lands in Calton.

Adeliza Carrou, relict of Gaufrid de Rotomago (Rheims) gave a house on the bridge at York.

Conan, Duke of Brittany and fifth Earl of Richmond, gave lands in Moulton, near Catterick.

Martin de Couton gave lands in Stapleton, near Moulton.

Ralph de Credeling, and Adam and Richard his sons, and Adam his grandson, gave lands, woods and minerals in Bradley.

Gaufrid, son of Stephen de Dromonby, gave lands in Dromonby.

Hugh de Eland gave lands in Elland, and pasturage in Exley.

Alan, son of Robert Rufus de Eseby, and Peter his son, gave lands in Eseby and Skipton on Swale.

William Fitz Duncan, son of Malcolm, King of Scotland, and Adeliza de Rumelli his wife, Baroness of Skipton, gave lands in Kilnsey.

Eustace Fitz John, lord of Knaresborough, gave lands in Cayton.

Arthur, son of Godard (A.D. 1151) gave lands in Bordley in Craven.

Roger, son of Roger de Grisetorpe, gave lands in Grisetorpe.

Agnes, Matilda and Avicia, daughters of Nigel Gurivant, gave lands in Kirkby Wiske.

Bertram Haget, a monk of Fountains, and brother of Ralph the Abbot, gave lands in Dacre.

William Haget gave lands in Caldwell, near Marton-le-Moor.

Nigel, sone of Gospatric de Hammerton, gave lands in Greenhammerton.

Richard de Hedune gave lands in Nutwith and Aldburgh, near Masham.

Baldwin, son of Ralph de Irton, gave lands in Dishforth, and a fishery in the river Swale.

Alan, son of Ketelli, gave lands in Kettlewell.

William, the son of Keter, gave lands in Sancton.

Edolphus de Kylnsay gave lands in Kilnsay.

Robert de Lacy, fourth Baron of Pontefract, gave pasturage in Marchdean.

John, son of Robert de Lanum, gave lands in Studley.

Thomas, son of Peter de Ledes, and Gilbert and William his sons, gave lands and minerals in Kirk Heaton.

'Annals of a Yorkshire Abbey' — William Grange, 1896
(the list is a selection only).

MANDATE FROM KING JOHN TO THE ABBEY OF FOUNTAINS

The King, to the Abbot or Prior of Fountains, greeting. We order you that, immediately when you have seen this letter, you send to us with utmost speed, by two of your monks and any others of your family in whom you place honest trust, everything of ours which you have in your keeping, new deposits as well as old, being vases, jewels, gold and silver, and anything else of ours which you have in your keeping, seeing that all these things may be brought to us safely and in secret; and when we have received them we will send you from here our letters of acquittance. Witnessed as above (at Windsor, June 24th., in the 17th year of our reign).

'Memorials of Fountains Abbey' — Surtees Society, Vol. 67 1876

The main doorway to the chapter house.

View through a window in the S. wall of the chapter house.

ON CROSSES, RELICS AND THE ORATORY LAMP

Let us have painted wooden crosses; let none of noteworthy size be of gold or silver. During special festivals, when relics are placed on the altar — which should happen only at mass, that is, on the feast of Holy Trinity and at all solemn masses in which there is a sermon in Chapter, apart from the first Sunday in Advent — let two wax candles be placed with them apart from the lights placed nearby. We should have whenever possible a lamp burning night and day in the Oratory.

ON GIFTS AND LETTERS

Concerning gifts, small presents and letters and eulogies, not to be given or received by any man without permission of his own abbot, let it be maintained completely as stated in the Rule. Transgressors should at least be whipped. Let the abbot consider the size and nature of the gift, and set the nature of the punishment accordingly.

ON PRISONS

In every abbey of our Order in which it is possible, let there exist strong and secure prisons where criminals may be thrown and detained at the abbot's discretion, according to the seriousness of their crimes. We call here 'criminals' those labouring under an unspeakable vice: thieves, arsonists, forgers, murderers. If an abbot should be a forger, let him be deposed.

ON NOVICES

Novices leaving their quarters, if they have been willing to return, are to do satisfaction as do other runaways. And if they are to be received, let them go to the hospice and there, be robed and come into the Chapter-house, and from the Chapter-house to probation. One who returns on the same day on which he left loses nothing from his rank. Novices who meet a leper on probation are lawfully excluded, but may be accommodated in the misericord; the same applies to epileptics.

Cistercian Statutes, 1256: 'Yorks. Arch. and Top. Journal', Vol.10 1886

The guest houses and the 12th C. bridge in a snow storm.

The same scene in spring, revealing the end of the lay-brothers' reredorter.

The first colony from Fountains was Newminster. In less than two years followed Kirkstead and Haverholme (afterwards removed to the neighbourhood of Louth). The latter house was established under Gervase as its first Abbot . . . In 1145 Abbot Murdoc supplied monks for De Bolbec, the founder of Woburn; and the next year a visit from Sigward, Bishop of Bergen, led to the settlement of thirteen monks from Fountains Abbey at Lysa in Norway. From Fountains, too, went Serlo, the chronicler, and eleven others under Alexander the Prior, to Bernoldswic, and eventually to Kirkstall, while only five days later Bytham (afterwards Vaudey) was added to the list. Finally in 1150, the Earl of Albermarle founded Meaux Abbey, with Adam, one of the original seceders from York, as its Abbot. Thus within twenty years Fountains became the mother of seven monasteries.

'The Ruined Abbeys of Yorkshire'
— W. C. Jefroy, 1891

THE FOUNDING OF KIRKSTALL

In the 1147th year from the incarnation of Our Lord, a noble, by name Henry de Lacy, undertook to build a monastery of the Cistercian Order in the Yorkshire region. He came, chose the spot, erected the monastery, and sent to it a convent of monks under Abbot Alexander. This Alexander was one of our first fathers, a brother in the womb of lord Richard, second Abbot of Fountains, who rested in peace, as has been said, at Clairvaux. Amongst these brothers I, Serlo, was sent, a man now in his dotage (as you can see for yourself) and broken by age. Our dwelling-place was at first called Bernolfwic,* but we, changing its name, called it St. Mary's Mount. We remained there for some years, suffering the discomforts of hunger and cold, both because of the inclement weather and because, through the unstable condition of the kingdom, our possessions were many times stolen by robbers. So we were unhappy with our home, and the abbey was converted into a grange. On the advice of our patron, we moved to another place called Kirkstall. In the fifteenth year after the foundation of Fountains, on July 15th, we were sent there under Abbot Alexander, twelve monks and ten lay brothers.

'The Fountains Chronicle' — Hugh of Kirkstall, 1207

* Barnoldswick

The Abbey from the south side. The wall running diagonally in the foreground is the E. wall of the monks' dormitory which contains much of the pre 1147 building. The dormitory was heightened later in the 12th C., and its new roof level is visible in the gable of the S. transept.

After the death of Archbishop Thurstan in 1140, great contention arose as to his successor. The court was in favour of William Fitzherbert, the treasurer of York, who was actually elected and consecrated. As there was some suspicion of his having used undue influence in securing his appointment, William encountered the most strenuous opposition from all the reformers of the day. The whole of the Cistercian order seem to have been banded against him, and among them were two abbots of Fountains, Richard and Murdac; the latter, indeed, seems to have led the opposition in England. He was a sufferer for what he did. In 1146, Pope Eugenius, instigated by St. Bernard, suspended William; and some of the Archbishop's kinsmen in England determined to wreak their vengence upon Murdac, whom they considered to be the chief agent in the degradation of their master. They made their way to Fountains with the intention of seizing the abbot. They could not find him; and in their rage broke open the gates, entered the church, ransacked the offices, pillaged the treasury, and then set fire to the monastery, and everything is said to have been consumed with the exception of a part of the oratory.

All the while Murdac was stretched in postrate adoration before the altar, expecting nothing but death every moment, but in the blindness of their fury they did not observe him. When the destroyers had departed he thankfully commenced the restoration of his house.

What was the real extent of the damages done, or the nature of the buildings destroyed cannot be determined. Whether their church was only a temporary erection or a substantial fabric of stone is not stated; the probability is that it was the latter; as they rose from poverty to comparative affluence in 1135, it is hardly likely that they would be settled eleven years without having erected a building which (internal fittings excepted) would suffer very little from fire. And we know that before 1145, they had received considerable funds for the erection of the abbey from Adam, son of Swain, a great land owner in South Yorkshire; their old friend Eustace Fitz John of Knaresborough Castle, and Alan, Earl of Richmond, who gave them a wood near Masham for that purpose.

'Annals of a Yorkshire Abbey' — William Grange, 1896

The entrance to the dormitory undercroft from the cloister. On the left can be seen the blocked doorway which led to an earlier 12th C. day-stairs and dormitory.

The doorway to the infirmary passage in the undercroft wall: the blocked doorway led into an earlier passage to the infirmary.

THE FIRE AT FOUNTAINS

They came to Fountains under arms, broke the door down, and in their arrogance entered the sanctuary, burst into the workshops and seized booty; not finding the Abbot, whom they sought, they reduced the sacred buildings, constructed with enormous labour, to cinders. They respected neither the order not the altar. They stood by, the holy convent, and watched the buildings erected by their own labour and spiritual suffering swept by flames and soon to become ashes. The only thing saved for them in all that disaster was the oratory with its attached workshops, preserved, as we believe, for use in prayers, and that half-burnt like a brand snatched from the fire. The Holy Abbot, prostrate at the foot of the altar, began to pray. No-one saw him, no-one harmed him; the hand of the Lord protected him. The troops left, their crime complete, taking their spoils with them: little money, but a wealth of condemnation. But the wicked did not rejoice in their impiety for long; the hand of the Lord lay heavily upon them. The blow of their enemy struck them down with cruel punishment and they died in their sins: some wasted by disease, some drowned in water, some turned to madness, others killed in different calamities, and mostly irreconciled. The Abbot and brothers, on the other hand, comforted in the Lord, their strength restored, as after a shipwreck resumed their voyage: they repaired the fallen, rebuilt the broken and, as it is written, 'the walls have fallen, but of squared stones' it was rebuilt. Faithful men from the region helped them, and the fabric rose again, far more splendid than it had been before.

'The Fountains Chronicle' — Hugh of Kirkstall, 1207

The mill bridge, early 13th C.

Sculptured capitals at the foot of the day-stairs in the cloister, 1160-80.

The nave in early sunlight, from scaffolding on the W. face. Originally this vista was broken by a rood screen, chapels and pulpitum: it was essentially two churches — W. end, lay-brothers and E. end, monks.

The typical Cistercian church, with its low elevation, its plain, bare walls, lighted by few windows and without stained glass, achieved its effect by the balance of masses and austere, powerful, round or pointed arches and mighty vaulting. These buildings filled anyone who entered them with peace and restfulness and disposed the soul for contemplation in an atmosphere of simplicity and poverty. St. Benedict's doctrine on humility, the basis of his teaching, was written out before them in stone.

'The Waters of Siloe' — Thomas Merton, 1950

How the Work of God is to be done in the Daytime

As the prophet said: 'Seven times in the day have I given praise to Thee'. And we shall observe this sacred number of seven if, at the times of Lauds, Prime, Tierce, Sext, None, Vespers and Compline, we fulfil the duties of our service. For it was of these hours of the day that he said: 'Seven times in the day have I given praise to Thee'; just as the same prophet saith of the night watches: 'At midnight I arose to give Thee praise'. At these times, therefore, let us sing the praises of our Creator for the judgements of His justice: that is, at Lauds, Prime, Tierce, Sext, None, Vespers and Compline: and at night let us rise to praise Him.

(Of those who come late to the Work of God or to table.)

As soon as the signal for the Divine Office has been heard, let them abandon what they have in hand and assemble with the greatest speed, yet soberly, so that no occasion be given for levity. Let nothing, therefore be put before the Work of God.

(Of the Divine Office at Night)

In winter time, that is, from the first of November until Easter, the brethren shall rise at what may be reasonably calculated to be the eighth hour of the night; so that having rested till some time past midnight, they may rise having had their full sleep. And let the time that remains after the Night-Office be spent in study by those brethren who have still some part of the psalter and lessons to learn. But from Easter to the first of November let the hour for the Night-Office be so arranged that, after a very short interval, during which the brethren may go out for the necessities of nature, Lauds, which are to be said at day-break, may begin without delay.

(Of those who make mistakes in the Oratory).

If any one make a mistake in the recitation of Psalm, Responsory, Antiphon, or Lesson, and do not humble himself by making satisfaction there before all, let him be subjected to severer punishment, as one who would not correct by humility what he did wrong through negligence. But children for such faults are to be whipt.

> Extracts from 'Rule of St. Benedict'
> — written 525-550

In the monks' quire in the abbey church of Fountains, and midway between the steps which remain on each side to mark the eastern limit of the stalls, lies a broken slab of grey marble, 9 feet 2 inches long, and 4 feet 7½ inches wide, with the casement of the brass of an abbot.

The brass seems to have represented the abbot in the ordinary habit of a Cistercian monk, the white tunic and cowl, holding a book in his left hand, and his crosier in his right. Above his head, but not on it, was a crocketed mitre without labels. The figure, which was 4 feet 7½ inches high, stood beneath a crocketed canopy with trefoiled arch, supported by pinnacled side shafts . . .

The slab at Fountains, according to Mr Walbran, was discovered in 1840 by some workmen employed in the abbey, who were anxious to find hidden treasure. Part of it was then taken up and found to cover a grave containing a skeleton.

The interest of the slab, apart from its having borne the brass of a Cistercian abbot, lies in the detached mitre . . . Its position on the slab, over instead of on the abbot's head, may be a piece of Cistercian humility, but it may also indicate that the abbot had ceased to wear it. Under what circumstances Abbot Greenwell's rule ended we do not know, but Thomas Swinton certainly resigned his office, and it is very likely that the slab is his.*

---

* John Greenwell, abbot, who ruled from 1442 to 1471, and Thomas Swinton, who was elected in 1471 but resigned in 1478-9.

> An article by M. Stephenson — Monumental Brasses in the West Riding: 'Yorks. Arch. Journal', Vol.15 1900

A marble slab at the crossing, once containing the brass of an abbot. (See opposite page.)

View into the presbytery from the S. transept, showing the original 12th C. arch, and below it Huby's arch (early 16th C.) added as support for an insecure central tower at the crossing.

Interior of the S. transept chapels: right, the original of 1150-60; left, the 15th C. extension breaking into the circular window.

By the excavation of the nave little information was obtained. In the urgent necessity to obtain space for the chantry chapels, it had been so divided and traversed by massy wooden screens, as to render the introduction of the larger windows on the south, and that noble one at the west end, a matter of necessity rather than of taste. Besides the chapels thus formed in the side aisles, the main body of the nave was crossed by not less than four screens, thus affording space for at least eight altars.

'Memorials of Fountains Abbey'
— Surtees Society, Vol.67 1876

Before we proceed to examine the church, it will be proper to state that the whole of its floor was excavated, or cleared of rubbish, during the winter of 1854 . . . The accumulation of rubbish varied in depth from little more than twelve inches, in the middle of the choir, to that of three feet in the nave. The whole mass appeared to have been disturbed, probably during Mr Aislabie's 'improvements', in the last century; so that, unfortunately, whatever fragmentary objects were found among it, could not be generally assigned to their original positions. There needed not, indeed, such an intrusion to disturb the last vestiges of evidence that might have been left; for the work had not proceeded far, before it became evident that, on the dissolution of the house, its spoliation had been conducted with no ordinary wantoness or avarice. The stalls, screens, and other wooden fittings, had, apparently, been used, as we *knew* was the case at Roche abbey, to make fires for melting the lead of the roofs; for, here and there were found, within the walls, heaps of ashes — nay, in the nave, part of the furnace where the operation had been conducted. All the glass had been removed from the windows, so that not more than a handful has been found. The large slabs had been torn from the graves and removed; nearly the whole of the tiled floor had been taken up; even the very graves had been ransacked in search of valuables, if we may judge from the condition of those that were accidently observed, and the indiscriminate mingling of bones with the rubbish.

'A Guide to Ripon and Fountains Abbey'
— J. R. Walbran, 1856

Nave and aisles delineated by snow — from Swanley Grange, north of the Abbey.

The extended presbytery, 1210-20: three of the five bays. The work is largely by Abbot John of Ely, 1211-1219, but it was begun by John of York and completed by John of Kent.

Psalm 51*

Have mercy upon me, O God, according to thy loving kindness: according unto the multitude of thy tender mercies blot out my transgressions.

2 Wash me throughly from mine iniquity, and cleanse me from my sin.

3 For I acknowledge my transgressions: and my sin *is* ever before me.

4 Against thee, thee only, have I sinned, and done *this* in thy sight: that thou mightest be justified when thou speakest, *and* be clear when thou judgest.

5 Behold, I was shapen in iniquity, and in sin did my mother conceive me.

6 Behold, thou desirest truth in the inward parts: and in the hidden *part* thou shalt make me to know wisdom.

7 Purge me with hyssop, and I shall be clean: wash me, and I shall be whiter than snow.

8 Make me to hear joy and gladness; *that* the bones *which* thou hast broken may rejoice.

9 Hide thy face from my sins, and blot out all mine iniquities.

10 Create in me a clean heart, O God; and renew a right spirit within me.

11 Cast me not away from thy presence; and take not thy holy spirit from me.

12 Restore unto me the joy of thy salvation; and uphold me *with thy* free spirit.

13 *Then* will I teach transgressors thy ways; and sinners shall be converted unto thee.

14 Deliver me from bloodguiltiness, O God, thou God of my salvation: *and* my tongue shall sing aloud of thy righteousness.

15 O Lord, open thou my lips; and my mouth shall shew forth thy praise.

16 For thou desirest not sacrifice; else would I give *it*: thou delightest not in burnt offering.

17 The sacrifices of God *are* a broken spirit: a broken and a contrite heart, O God, thou wilt not despise.

18 Do good in thy good pleasure unto Zion: build thou the walls of Jerusalem.

19 Then shalt thou be pleased with the sacrifices of righteousness, with burnt offering and whole burnt offering: then shall they offer bullocks upon thine altar.

* Sung by Cistercians on their way to church after the main meal of the day.

The Chapel of the Nine Altars and the presbytery at the beginning of Spring: the view is from Swanley Grange.

The process of excavation was commenced at the south end of the Lady Chapel. This place was not used for the general services of the church; but was divided by a high wooden screen that ran, longitudinally, down the centre, and by others that were joined to it at one end and the eastern wall at the other, into nine compartments or chapels, in each of which was an altar, dedicated to some particular saint, at which daily prayers were said for the souls of certain persons deceased, who had endowed a chaplain for that purpose. Of these altars, portions of six have been discovered; the rest having, no doubt, been destroyed when Mr Aislabie erected the absurd gallery under the great eastern window. Two of them remain in tolerable perfection; but in all the cases, the covering slabs have been removed. The pavement of the chapel has been utterly destroyed, with the exception of some plain work near the south door, that had been inserted not long before the Reformation. If a conjecture might be suggested by some small fragments of pot-metal glass that were found here, some or all of the lancet windows might have retained their original glazing to the last. Of the immense quantity of glass that filled the great eastern window, it is strange to say that not one particle was observed. As, however, at the time of the Reformation, even plain glass was so costly, that it was often fixed in wooden frames, and removed from the windows when the apartments were not in occupation, and this window had not then been erected much more than fifty years, it is very probable that this, and the rest of the glass that was marketable, was at once removed and sold.

When I found that the pavement of the Lady Chapel had been thus mercilessly destroyed, and that no sepulchral memorials were to be found in its chantry chapels, I watched, with some curiosity, the removal of the rubbish between the high altar and the east window; where I sought thirteen years ago, for the memorial of Abbot Gower, who I knew was interred in this particular spot in 1390. The search was at that time unsuccessful; but I found, within two feet of the sward, *and above the level of the old pavement*, the skeleton of a man, who, since his skull was decapitated and placed on his breast, must unquestionably have suffered a violent death, and have been buried here, after the dissolution of the house, and the present formation of the rubbish; and that the more decidedly, since the body laid north and south, evincing unchristian burial. Exposure to the air had, however, wrought its usual effect on this irrevocable mystery, and, with the exception of some few fragments, no part of the skeleton could be found.

'Memorials of Fountains Abbey' — Surtees Society, Vol. 42 1862.
An address by J. R. Walbran on the 1851 excavations.

The Chapel of the Nine Altars looking north: it was built under Abbot John of Kent, 1220-1247.

A double piscina in the S. wall of the Chapel of the Nine Altars.

The first, or Trans.-Norm. *choir*, was aisleless, short, and narrow. Its foundations are traced by lines of flagstones within the present choir, which was begun by Abbot John of York (de Ebor — 1203-1211), continued by John of Hessle (1211-1219) and completed by Abbot John of Kent (1220-1247). The design is simple, yet very graceful, E. Eng. Some tesselated pavement remains before the site of the high altar. But the choir, however graceful, must have yielded in beauty to the *Chapel of the Nine Altars*, an eastern transept, which was also the work of Abbot John of Kent. A similar eastern transept, bearing the same name, was added to Durham Cathedral nearly at the same time, and Peterborough Cathedral has a transept of Perp. date, in the same position. The want of space for shrines and altars compelled these additions. Fountains indeed was never fortunate enough to procure the relics of any distinguished saint, although great efforts were made to obtain those of St. Robert of Knaresborough, who died whilst this transept was building; but the abbey possessed lesser relics, and altar-room was much required. The E. Eng. work here is plain and massive, but the general design is of great beauty; the lofty arches, in line with the choir-arcade, giving much peculiar character; and the view, looking across the transept, from S. to N., is especially to be noticed. The great E. window was a Perp. insertion. The grey marble, which was used plentifully here and in the choir (although the greater part has disappeared), was procured by the monks from their own lands in Nidderdale.

Murray's 'Handbook for Travellers in Yorkshire' — 1882

The chapel is 117 feet in length, and is divided by two arcades which were in a line with those of the presbytery. The pillars, about 50 feet high, are octagonal, and were surrounded by eight marble shafts. The arches of the arcades are the work of Darnton, who probably found the church in a state of bad repair. He took down the stone vaults of this chapel and the presbytery and the upper part of the arch between them, and replaced them by an open roof of wood. You can still see the horizontal wall courses of the springers of the vaults which he left after he had removed the mouldings.

That the vault of the chapel was in a dangerous condition may be surmised from the settlement of two of the windows, the most northern on the east side and the most eastern on the south side. Darnton repaired the settlement of the first window by inserting carved stones.*

'The Ruins of Fountains Abbey'
— Rev. A. W. Oxford, 1910

* (see pages 74 & 171)

The Chapel of the Nine Altars and the presbytery, in mid-winter.

The chapel of the Nine Altars: a carving inserted by Darnton to mend a fracture, circa 1483. From below upwards:- an angel holding a shield, an abbot's head, a scroll between two fishes, and a figure of St. James the Great.

The centre three altars in the Chapel of the Nine Altars, with aumbries set in the wall. At a later date the three altars were combined to make one, standing under the great window.

Royalty, the nobility, bishops, abbots, deans, lords of the manor, and wealthy merchants in their turn sought such spiritual and posthumous benefits as the endowment of a chantry would confer upon them. In general, the endowment took the form of lands, tenements, rents, and other possessions, and sometimes of money. It provided a stipend for the priest whose office was to sing masses periodically for the founder and for 'all the faithful departed' at a special altar in a church or in a chantry chapel; and frequently part of the endowment was set aside to bestow a weekly dole upon the poor . . . A moderate endowment would ensure the recitation of masses on the first, third, seventh, and thirtieth day after the death of the testator, with an obit, i.e. a mass that was sung on the anniversary for a few years or in perpetuity, a provision that seemed to be the most frequently favoured.

In the churches of Cistercian abbeys, from which the laity were wholly excluded, an array of chantry chapels might not be looked for. Benedictine abbots had their chapels and tombs, but the heads of Cistercian houses contented themselves with a slab in the pavement of cloister or chapter house. That is not to say that soul-masses and obits were not sung in their churches; chantries were founded and anniversaries of patrons and benefactors were duly observed at their altars.

The great eastern transept of the nine altars at Fountains abbey and the range of eight chapels flanking the nave of Melrose were built to meet the need of more and more altars for soul-masses in those Cistercian churches.

'Medieval Chantries and Chantry Chapels'
— G. H. Cook, 1963

The west guest house (1160-80) showing the privy on two levels in a turret over the Skell.

In the old days of the abbey the guest-houses (Hospitia) were of great importance. The rule of St. Benedict prescribed that all guests who came should be received as Christ himself — *Omnes supervenientes hospites tanquam Christus suscipiantur.* The arrival at the outer gate was reported to the abbot, who came to meet the guest and then took him into the little chapel* for prayer before bringing him through the inner gate into the monastery.

'The Ruins of Fountain Abbey'
— Rev. A. W. Oxford, 1910.

* This was between the outer W. gate and the present entrance: there are no remains.

The guest houses stand in what was once a walled courtyard occupying the bend of the river west of the lay-brothers' infirmary. There are substantial remains of two of them, both built shortly after the middle of the 12th Century, and they are amongst the best examples in Britain of a particular type of stone dwelling house that is also found in towns, on manors, and as domestic accommodation within castles during the 12th and 13th Centuries. Each is a simple rectangular building of two storeys, with a hall, chamber and privy on each floor. In the 12th century therefore, they were capable of providing four complete and independent sets of accommodation for important visitors and their travelling households.

. . . Ambitious as they are, these surviving guest-houses only formed part of a larger group. Excavation showed that other buildings had stood to the north-west, extending as far as the river bank where a pair of massive corbels for a latrine remains in the river wall.*

The Fountains Abbey Guide Book
— R. Gilyard-Beer, 1970

* (see page 148).

The interior of the lower level of the privy in the west guest house.

The task of affording hospitality was a burden that fell with particular weight on the Yorkshire houses. Their location, of course, had much to do with this. There were relatively few religious houses in Yorkshire; several of these were too small and others were not so willing to render hospitality. The Cistercian houses were nearly all large and were situated on some of the main highways; these facts, added to their reputation, attracted many travellers. It is rather a mistake to dwell on the inaccessibility of the Yorkshire houses. While it is true that they sought out-of-the-way places for their foundations, several things conspired to break down their isolation once the foundation was made.

A Visitor of high rank usually brought a very large retinue which taxed the capacity even of the larger houses, and if their stay was at all extended, as it often was, the expense was great. It is estimated that when the king spent three nights in Oxfordshire on one occasion the cost was £150. . . . In 1322, Edward II, on a Scotch campaign, stopped at Rievaulx and during the next year stopped at Jervaulx. It was not an uncommon thing for nobles to spend months in some monastery or other.

In offering hospitality to travelers, especially to those prominent, more than mere lodging had to be provided. The guests had to be entertained, especially if their visits were prolonged, and special articles of food had to be provided for them. In many of the accounts we find bills for wines, pears, partridges, sprats, fish of all sorts, spices, figs, raisins, etc., etc. Salley, the poorest of the Yorkshire houses, spent twenty-seven shillings four pence for minstrels in 1381. The list of items for entertainment at Fountains included minstrels from six to eight pence each (sixteen items); a fool from Byland, at four pence; players from Thirsk, twelve pence; Simon, a fool, four pence; players of Ripon, two shillings; a strange fabulist, six pence; a servant with shellfish, twenty pence; the king's minstrels, six shillings eight pence; the boy-bishop of Ripon, three shillings.

It is not surprising to find such a long list of entertainers at an abbey such as Fountains. It was favourably located and large enough to accommodate any group of travelers. Undoubtedly it had a wide reputation for hospitality.

'A History of the Work of the Cistercians in Yorkshire'
— F. A. Mullins, 1932

The guest houses at snowdrop time.

The guest houses in mid-winter.

Windows and clustered columns in the E. guest house.

THE GUEST-MASTER

By the time the Order has become permanently settled he is a personage of considerable importance . . . He must be a man who always has his wits about him, who is gifted with tact, discretion and politeness, who is neither garrulous nor taciturn, but knows how to converse readily and wisely with those whom he entertains. He is to make sure the guest house is ready for the reception of visitors; that lights, fire, warm water, clean linen, rushes for the floors, and writing materials are provided, and that the cellarer is notified as to food. He is to receive guests as he would receive Our Lord, assuring them of welcome, putting them at their ease, personally assuring himself that everything is done for their comfort. He is also to explain the rules of the house, to arrange for the attendance at church if the guest so desires, and if the guest be a person of consequence, to acquaint the abbot with his presence. He is to speed his parting as he is to welcome his coming, taking care that nothing is left behind in the guest chambers, and that the God-speed of the brotherhood goes with the visitor.

'Cistercians in Yorkshire' — J. S. Fletcher, 1919

The 12th C. bridge leading to the east guest house: note the 12th C. circular window blocked in the 14th C. to allow for the flue of a fire immediately below it.

How the Monks are to sleep

Let them sleep each one in a separate bed, receiving bedding suitable to their manner of life, as the Abbot shall appoint. If possible, let all sleep in one place: but if the number do not permit of this, let them repose by tens or twenties with the seniors who have charge of them. Let a candle burn constantly in the cell until morning. Let them sleep clothed, and girded with belts or cords — but not with knives at their sides, lest perchance they wound themselves in their sleep — and thus be always ready, so that when the signal is given they may rise without delay, and hasten each to forestall the other in going to the Work of God, yet with all gravity and modesty. Let not the younger brethren have their beds by themselves, but among those of the seniors. And when they rise for the Work of God, let them gently encourage one another, because of the excuses of the drowsy.

On clothes

For their bedding let a straw mattress, blanket, coverlet, and pillow suffice. These beds must be frequently inspected by the Abbot, to see if any private property be discovered therein. And if any one should be found to have anything which he hath not received from the Abbot, let him be subjected to the most severe discipline. In order that this vice of private ownership may be rooted out entirely, let the Abbot supply them with all necessaries: that is, a cowl, tunic, shoes, stockings, girdle, knife, pen, needle, handkerchief, and tablets . . .

'Rule of St. Benedict' — 525-550

View from the bank S. of the Abbey showing: right, the pillars of the undercroft to the monks' dormitory; l. warming house with its wood-yard, and muniment room above. Originally the river extended up to the wal foreground.

A view from inside the undercroft, showing alternately small and large windows in the dormitory (see opposite): low down, right, is a blocked window of the earlier dormitory (pre 1147 fire) and left is a blocked archway used in the later 12th C. rebuilding.

The part of the dormitory over the chapter house had its floor at a higher level than the rest, and was lit by round-headed windows spaced some 15ft apart. The rest of the dormitory had similar but larger windows spaced from 18 to 21ft apart, with smaller rectangular windows between.

In a monastic dormitory the beds were usually placed against the side walls, leaving a central space in which, at Clairvaux, stood great wardrobes for the monks' clothes. In some houses it was the practice to place the beds of the novices between those of the monks, for better supervision, and the alternating types of windows here at Fountains may be a sign of this. Later in the Middle Ages, to keep pace with increasing demands for more privacy, dormitories were usually divided into cubicles by wooden partitions, and some of the holes in the walls between the windows here may have been for that purpose. Another late alteration was the insertion of a narrow doorway in the south wall of the projection over the chapter house, from which a bridge led to the upper storey of the infirmary gallery.

Fountains Abbey Guide Book
— R. Gilyard-Beer, 1970

THE CHAMBERLAIN.— The chamberlain's office was domestic. With the exception of food, his department included all matters relating to the comfort and well-being of the convent. He and his assistant had the care of the dorter. He provided straw for the mattresses once a year, when the opportunity was taken for a thorough cleaning. He was to provide warm water for shaving and soap for washing the heads of the brethren, also baths, for which he had to buy the wood for heating the water. Baths were taken three or four times a year, and he bought sweet hay to spread round the tubs for the brethren to stand on. Hot water was also required for feet-washing on Saturdays, and a good fire had to be kept in the calefactory. The heads of the monks were shaved every three weeks. They sat silently in two rows in the cloister facing each other; the elder monks, were treated first, and by the time the water was cool and towels wet the turn of the novices came.

The chamberlain's principal work was the providing of clothes for the brethren. The tailory was under his charge and 'he should provide tailors, trustworthy, sober, unassuming, secret, not talkative, nor drunken, or lying, as they were summoned into the interior privacy of the monastery, where they could hear and see the secrets of the brethren. Such men should not be lightly engaged nor lightly discharged. The tailor should know exactly the shape and cut of the brethren's woollen and linen garments. These should be neither sumptuous nor sordid.' At Branwell every canon had an outfit once a year, but at Westminster the brethren were served in rotation. He also looked after the repairs; in one of the Custumals any monk who wanted a garment repaired placed it in the morning in one of the bays of the cloister, where it was collected and replaced when mended. He bought the cloth and skins required, either by interview or from the fairs. He was to find a laundress of good reputation and character to wash the linen, surplices, rochets, sheets, shirts and drawers; these were washed once a fortnight in summer and once in three weeks in winter. Great care was to be taken that no losses occurred and all articles were entered on tallies and returned in the same way. He looked after the boots and was supplied with pigs' fat from the kitchen three times a year to make grease to keep the leather supple. The sub-chamberlain was to supply the lamps for the dorter, to light them and extinguish them. Illustrating the exact division of duties between the various officers, the sacrist supplied the dorter bell, but the cord came from the chamberlain. The sub-almoner provided the needles, but the sub-chamberlain the thread.

'The English Abbey' — F. H. Crossley, 1935

The southernmost chapel was cleared out in 1849, and shows nothing upon the floor, except a slightly elevated altar-platform, and some small fragments of geometrical pavement that adhere to the walls.

Abutting on the western wall of this wing of the transept, was found the base of a staircase, that formerly led to the vestry or sacristy.* Of the situation of this apartment, which is entirely inaccessible to any one who has any respect for their comfort or their bones, you may derive the best idea from the knowledge that it is immediately above that dark vaulted passage intervening between the south transept and the chapter-house, where many paving tiles were formerly strewn about, and a place generally described by the guides as the 'bone-house'; wherein, as I will mention anon, they spoke more truth than they intended. On clearing out this apartment, there was nothing remarkable observed, with the exception of a lavatory in the south wall, under a well-moulded semicircular arch — in fact a sink where the vessels used in the church were washed; but in the olden time, the interest and value of its contents must have been extreme, for here were deposited the most valued treasures with which four centuries of wealthy patrons and benefactors had endeavoured to testify the devotion of their faith, and to dignify the ceremonials of the house . . .

Below the vestry* is a long, narrow, vaulted passage, leading from the cloister court to the burial ground, on the south side of the choir. The doorways at each end have long been walled up, so as to form the place into a gloomy apartment, formerly filled with tesseræ and paving tiles. In the course of the excavation, however, it became necessary to take down the wall which separated it from the cloister court; and then, under rubbish that had fallen from the vaulted roof above, was discovered a mass of human bones, sufficient, according to a careful computation, to have formed not less than four hundred skeletons. When they were torn from faithless graves, or gathered, after barbarous exposure, by some friendly hands into this common tomb, is now entirely forgotten. They were removed, on the day when they were found, to a grave prepared for them, at the west end of the nave; and, during the process of removal, I could not refrain, in most vivid retrospection of the imposing treasures of gold and silver and jewels that were so long hoarded but a few feet above, and of the richly decorated robes of state in which many of these once consecrated bones were invested, from reflecting, with Jeremy Taylor, that it was 'a copy of the greatest change from rich to naked — from ceiled roofs to arched coffins — from living like gods to dying like men;' and from feeling, in the memorable words used by Sir Thomas Browne in his 'Hydriotaphia,' that they were 'vain ashes, that, in the oblivion of times, persons, names, and sexes, had formed to themselves a fruitless continuation, and only arise unto late posterity as emblems of mortal vanities.'

'Memorials of Fountains Abbey' — Surtees Society, Vol 67, 1876. (J. R. Walbran)

* now referred to as the treasury (see page 90).

The S. wall of the S. transept. The doorway high on the right leads to the monks' dormitory (from stairs now missing). The lower doorway leads to the sacristy and to stairs in the transept wall: above this is the built-in doorway to an earlier 12th C. dormitory.

The doorway of the treasury: the treasury lies above the passage between the S. transept and the chapter house.

The passage between the S. transept and the chapter house: the half barrel vault at the top of the picture supports the night stairs to the dormitory above.

Of the Daily Manual Labour

After their meal, let them occupy themselves in their reading, or in learning the Psalms. During Lent, let them apply themselves to reading from morning until the end of the third hour, and then, until the end of the tenth, labour at whatever is enjoined them. And in these days of Lent, let each one receive a book from the library, and read it all through in order. These books are to be given out at the beginning of Lent. Above all, let one or two seniors be appointed to go round the Monastery, at the hours when the brethren are engaged in reading, and see that there be no slothful brother giving himself to idleness or to foolish talk, and not applying himself to his reading, so that he is thus not only useless to himself, but a distraction to others. If such a one be found (which God forbid) let him be corrected once and a second time; and if he do not amend, let him be subjected to the chastisement of the Rule, so that the rest may be afraid. And let not one brother associate with another at unreasonable hours.

On Sunday, let all occupy themselves in reading, except those who have been appointed to the various offices. But if any one should be so negligent and slothful, as to be either unwilling or unable to study or to read, let some task be given him to do, that he be not idle. To brethren who are weak or delicate, let there be given such work or occupation as to prevent them either from being idle, or from being so oppressed by excessive labour as to be discouraged. Their weakness must be taken into account by the Abbot.

'Rule of St. Benedict', 525-550

Since the monks lived in the cloister, all the buildings connected with their daily life are placed round it, and accessible from it. These buildings were enumerated in their proper order in the directions in the *Consuetudines* for the Sunday procession, as follows: *capitulum* or chapter-house, *auditorium* or parlour, *dormitorium* or dorter, *dormitorii necessaria* or rere-dorter, *calefactorium* or warming house, *refectorium* or frater, *coquina* or kitchen, *cellarium* or cellarer's building.

On Sunday mornings, after the blessing of the holy water before high mass, the whole community, under the direction of the precentor, left the choir in procession and visited and sprinkled with holy water all the buildings round the cloister in the following order: capitulum, auditorium, etc. — (as in above quotation).

'The Ruins of Fountains Abbey'
— Rev. A. W. Oxford, 1910

The cloister viewed from the top of the west face of the nave: in the centre is the warming house chimney, and to the right, the refectory and kitchen.

The west face of the church and the lay brothers' range seen on a winter's day.

MEMBERS OF CONVENT NOT TO BE SENT TO GRANGES.

There is a restriction on the sending of the convent at harvest-time to stay overnight at granges, unless through unavoidable necessity. And monks who are ill in the head will be able to be retained in hood and scapula, separate in the abbey or granges as the abbot may see fit. Monks and lay brothers will not be allowed to have blood let except in abbeys of our Order, unless through great and obvious need; and unless they may be in Rome or living permanently with cardinals, archbishops or bishops. Lay brothers bled in the abbey are to leave after their meal on the third day.

Cistercian Statute, 1256: 'Yorks. Arch. & Top. Journal', Vol. 10 1886

A footnote by J. T. Fowler

It was a matter of course to be bled from time to time, some Orders having no set times, but generally avoiding Lent and great festivals, while others had fixed times, from four to six or more times a year. The operation was performed by the 'minutor'[1] of the Abbey, in the Common-house,[2] before a good fire, and 'special consolations in food and drink' were provided for the patients, with other relaxations of the rigour of their ordinary mode of life. The Cistercian bleeding times were in February, April, September, and about St. John's Day, (i.e. probably in December, after Christmas), and a bleeding was so far a holiday that to 'lose' it was a punishment.[3]

[1] 'minutor' — technical term for the physician qualified to perform bleeding.
[2] a term for the warming-house.
[3] see also page 135.

The fireplace in the warming house: note the lintel of 'joggled' stones — i.e. fitted together in such a way as to be immovable if shaken.

Of the Clothes and Shoes of the Brethren

Let clothing be given to the brethren suitable to the nature and the climate of the place where they live: for in cold countries more is required, in warm countries less. This must therefore be considered by the Abbot. We think, however, that in temperate climates a cowl and a tunic should suffice for each monk: the cowl to be of thick stuff in winter, but in summer something worn or thin: likewise a scapular for work, and shoes and stockings to cover their feet. And let not the Monks complain of the colour or coarseness of these things, but let them be such as can be got in the country where they live, or can be bought most cheaply.

Let the Abbot be careful about the size of the garments, that they be not too short for those who wear them, but of the proper length. When they receive new clothes, let them always give up the old ones at once, to be put by in the wardrobe for the poor. For it is sufficient for a monk to have two tunics and two cowls, for wearing at night and also for washing: whatever is over and above this is superfluous, and ought to be cut off. In the same way, let them give up their shoes, and whatever else is worn out, when they receive new ones. Let those who are sent on a journey receive drawers from the wardrobe, and on their return restore them washed. Their cowls and tunics also, which are to be a little better than those they ordinarily wear, let them receive from the wardrobe when setting out on their journey, and give them back on their return.

'Rule of St. Benedict', 525-550

Outside the warming-house, on the south, is a yard between the frater and the dorter range, with a wall on the river bank. On the east side of it was a building of the same date as the warming-house, 30 feet long and about 13 feet wide, with an entrance from the yard. It had a vaulted roof and a chamber above, and was probably a store for wood and fuel for the warming-house fires. Along the frater wall was a pentise from the warming-house as far as the cutwater at the end of the frater, and a plank bridge was carried from the yard wall to the cutwater across the arm of the stream which here runs under the frater.

The plank bridge probably continued across the main stream to the opposite bank, to bring fuel over.

Fountains Abbey — St. John Hope: 'Yorks. Arch. Journal', Vol.15 1898

The south doorway and pointed windows of the warming house, 1180-1210.

THE FRATERER.— His duties were in the refectory. He laid the tablecloths and had them washed and repaired, and provided new ones when necessary. He poured the beer into jugs, which were to be washed inside and out once a week. He was also to produce after dinner two jugs of beer for the convent and its guests, one freshly drawn, but the other filled with the liquor left from the other jugs. He washed the cups and spoons every day and kept a tally of them. He also fetched the bread from the cellar, and was not to offer it if it had been gnawed by mice. When the bread was laid on the tables it was to be properly covered up. The fraterer provided the mats and rushes to strew the floor and the alleyways of the cloister near the frater door. He was to clean the frater thoroughly with besoms as often as this was required. In summer he threw flowers, mint and fennel into the air to make a sweet odour and he also provided fans. In winter he was to supply candles for the tables. If a brother sat by himself he had a candle, but if two or three sat together, they were only to have one candle between them.

The fraterer had charge of the lavatory, and was to remove any dirt or dregs lying in the bottom of it, so that the brethren might have clean water for washing their hands and faces. He was to keep sand and a whetstone always ready to clean, and sharpen the knives, and to provide clean towels. The furniture of the frater was simple, but at Westminster it possessed valuable plate, the gifts of the brethren and the King. The frater at Durham was supplied with silver-plate, kept in an aumbry by the frater door. 'Every monk had his mazer severally to himself that he did drink in, and they were all largely and finely edged with silver about them and double gilt with gold.' It was a rule that anyone drinking should hold the cup with both hands as a sign of humility; during excavation in the Yorkshire Cistercian abbeys a few two-handled cups were found.*

'The English Abbey' — F. H. Crossley, 1935

* Some are in the museum at Fountains.

Stairs to the pulpit in the refectory, 118

The monks' refectory: behind it lies the S. end of the lay-brothers' range (their refectory) lying over the Skell. The river, now narrower through silting, originally ran through the arch which can be seen under the last bay of the refectory.

The sculptured corbel carrying the reading pulpit in the refectory.

Of the Measure of Drink

Every one hath his proper gift from God, one after this manner, another after that. And therefore it is with some misgiving that we appoint the measure of other men's living. Yet, considering the infirmity of the weak, we think that one pint of wine a day is sufficient for each: but let those to whom God gives the power of abstinence know that they shall have their proper reward. If, however, the situation of the place, the work, or the heat of summer require more, let it be in the power of the Superior to grant it; taking care at all times that surfeit or drunkenness creep not in. And although we read that wine ought by no means to be the drink of Monks, yet since in our times Monks cannot be persuaded of this, let us at least agree not to drink to satiety, but sparingly: because 'wine maketh even the wise to fall away'. But where the necessity of the place alloweth not even the aforesaid measure, but much less, or none at all, let those who dwell there bless God, and not murmur. This above all we admonish, that there be no murmuring among them.

Of the Measure of Food

We think it sufficient for the daily meal, whether at the sixth or the ninth hour, that there be at all seasons of the year two dishes of cooked food, because of the weakness of different people; so that he who perchance cannot eat of the one, may make his meal of the other. Let two dishes, then, suffice for all the brethren; and if there be any fruit or young vegetables, let a third be added. Let one pound weight of bread suffice for the day, whether there be but one meal, or both dinner and supper. If they are to sup, let a third part of the pound be kept back by the Cellarer, and given to them for supper. If, however, their work chance to have been hard, it shall be in the Abbot's power, if he thinks fit, to make some addition, avoiding above everything all surfeiting, that the Monks be not overtaken by indigestion. For there is nothing so adverse to a Christian as gluttony, according to the words of our LORD: 'See that your hearts be not over-charged with surfeiting'. And let not the same quantity be allotted to children of tender years, but less than to their elders, moderation being observed in every case. Let every one abstain altogether from the flesh of four-footed animals, except the very weak and the sick.

'Rule of St. Benedict', 525-550

The frater was arranged with a table at the end opposite the door, and others on each side against the walls. At meal times the tables were covered with linen cloths, and the cellarer and cooks who waited on their brethren ought to have had everything necessary on the tables before they came in. About in the middle of the west wall was the pulpit for the reader.

The prior generally presided in the frater, as the abbot had to entertain the guests, but if there was no guests the abbot was to dine with the others.

After the preceding hour had been sung, if the dinner was ready, the prior gave the signal, and all went to the laver and washed their hands, after which they entered the frater. If, however, the dinner was not ready, he waited until it was, the monks meanwhile sitting at their books in the cloister. Each man as he entered the frater bowed towards the high table, and then stood by his seat till the prior came; or, if he were late, which he was specially enjoined not to be, men sat and rose up at his coming. The prior on taking his place rang a little bell for a time, and then the priest for the week blessed the meal, the convent joining in the responses. When they were sat down the reader began, and the prior gave the signal to the rest by uncovering his bread.

The behaviour of the monks at table is carefully ordered in the *consuetudines*, and the passage is curious from the view it gives us of the customs of polite society in the first half of the twelfth century. No one has to leave the room during the meal, nor to walk about whilst eating. He was not to wash his cup with his fingers, but he might wipe it if he liked. He might not wipe his hands or his knife on the table-cloth unless he first cleaned them on his bread. He was to help himself to salt with his knife, and when he drank he was to hold the cup with both his hands.

At the end of the meal the prior stopped the reader and rang his bell, at the sound of which all rose and went in order, singing the fifty-first Psalm on the way, to the church, and there returned thanks.

The reader and those who had served at table dined after the others, one of them presiding, and the same forms being observed as with the convent. But to all those who, by reason of their service, had to dine thus late, an extra allowance called *mixtum* was given on all days except the week-days of Lent, the rogation and ember days, and certain vigils. *Mixtum* was to each man a quarter of a pound of bread and a third of a measure of drink, — perhaps half a pint, — and it was taken in the frater before or after sext, as the day might be. The younger men were also allowed *mixtum*, which they took before terce.

The Cistercian Order — an article by J. T. Micklethwaite: 'Yorkshire Archaeological Journal', Vol.15 1900

The S. walk of the cloister, E. end, seen from the lay-brothers' dormitory: left to right — doorway into infirmary passage, warming house, refectory, kitchen. The lavatory or laver runs along the length of the wall.

Most of the lower part of the south wall of the cloister is occupied by the lavatory. This is divided into two parts by the frater door. The western half, which is the more perfect of the two, has a pointed arch in the middle, with two round arches on each side, originally supported by marble pillars, all now lost, but their section may be recovered from the curious sockets cut out for the end pillars. The pillars stood on a broad bench, with a lead or stone trough below, so contrived that the monks could stand in front to wash their hands, and get up and sit on the bench with their feet in the trough for the usual Saturday *mandatum* or foot-washing. The trough was supplied with water from a pipe in the middle, which came up through the bench, and had a branch through the wall into the corner of the frater. The overflow ran off under the trough, and was carried away by a down pipe.

Fountains Abbey — St. John Hope: 'Yorks. Arch. Journal', Vol.15 1898

Every Saturday, during collation, the feet of all the monks in turn were washed by those who had served as cooks for the week and those who were to do so for the coming week. This was the weekly maundy, and it must not be confounded with the ceremony of Maundy Thursday in commemoration of our Lord's washing of the feet of the Apostles, which was observed in Cistercian abbeys as it was in other places.

J. T. Micklethwaite — (as page 102)

Of those who come late to the Work of God or to table

If any one, through his own negligence and fault, come not to table before the Verse, so that all may say this and the prayer together, and together sit down to table, let him be once or twice corrected. If after this he do not amend, let him not be admitted to share in the common table, but be separated from the companionship of all, and eat alone, his portion of wine being taken from him, until he hath made satisfaction and amends. Let him be punished in like manner, who is not present also at the Verse which is said after meals. And let no one presume to take food or drink before or after the appointed hour: but should a brother be offered anything by the Superior, and refuse to take it, if he afterwards desire either what he before refused, or anything else, he shall receive nothing whatever, until he hath made proper satisfaction.

'Rule of St. Benedict', 525-550

View from the top of the staircase in the S. transept wall: left to right — roof of the muniment room, refectory, kitchen, lay-brothers' dormitory, reredorter and infirmary, pigeons, and in the distance the bakehouse and malthouse ('northern and southern industrial buildings').

The moulded doorway leading into the refectory, 1180-1210.

The Cistercians did not conceive penance as a system of arbitary practices by which the abbot could tease his monks. The penitential life of the White Monk did not consist in a series of athletic feats of endurance or of systematic flagellations, or even of deliberately-staged public humiliations. The Cistercians were basing their life on the Gospel: and the 'austerity' of the life that was led and preached by Jesus Christ is the broad, fundamental, searching austerity of labour and poverty. The penance of the Cistercians is essentially the common penance of the whole human race: to 'eat your bread in the sweat of your brow' and to 'bear one another's burdens.' There would be plenty of cold and hunger and insecurity. Night after night the monk would go to his simple bed of straw, under the stone vaulting of his unheated dormitory, to rest his aching muscles for a few hours. He would rise in the middle of the night and pray and work for a good long time before he got anything to put into his empty stomach. He would know the heat of the sun. His hands would be hard and rough from field work or building or the exercise of a craft.

It must not be imagined that these monks simply indulged in such things out of pious fancy. The poverty and labour of the early Cistercians had explicit reference to the social situation in which they lived. Besides being a return to St. Benedict and the Gospel, their way of life was also a protest against the inordinate wealth of so many of the great feudal abbeys.

'The Waters of Siloe' — Thomas Merton, 1950

A panoramic view from the malthouse (southern industrial buildings).

PITTANCES NOT TO BE SOUGHT AFTER

On pittances,* let the old order be maintained, that on no day in any circumstances may they be awaited as if by custom or right, nor may there be any unless by the judgement of the Abbot. A monk or lay brother who requests a pittance in breach of this regulation is to be punished in the chapter-house by the judgement of the president. A monk or lay brother who suggests to any lay person that alms which he would wish to give to the Abbot he may give to the convent especially for a pittance will do without pittance for a month, unless he is ill or has been bled.

PRIORS NOT TO OWN PROPERTY

Priors of the Order are not to own sheep, mantles, spurs or anything at all of their own, nor are they to involve themselves to any extent in rents and alms gathered to provide pittances for the convents; everything should be apportioned at the Abbot's will. Priors who transgress this instruction are to be deposed. In addition, let them not take it upon themselves to give anything at all, neither the Priors themselves nor the cellarers nor the other officers of the house, against the order or prohibition of their own abbot. Anyone who transgress is to be on bread and water, every sixth day as long as his abbot wishes.

Cistercian Statutes, 1256 — 'Yorks. Arch. and Top. Journal', Vol.10 1886

* footnote in the above Journal by J. T. Fowler

Extra commons or allowance over and above the ordinary fare, served at the end of a meal in the prater. Pittances were provided by benefactors and distributed to the monks on particular days. It is said that at first they were of the value of one *picta*, a very small coin of Poictou, to each person. The word, however, occurs as *pietantia*, and is perhaps quite as likely to be connected with 'piety'. It is one of those words which have 'come down in the world,' and its modern use may well have arisen out of monks being dissatisfied with their 'pittances'. At Newminster there were endowments for pittances of bread, good ale, and salmon, on the anniversaries of the donors' deaths, the idea being that pious monks would be moved by gratitude to pray for their souls.

The inner north wall of the kitchen showing the entrance and beam holes.

Monastic meals, though monotonous, were wholesome; and there was a good deal of variety in the preparation of the fish. St. Bernard complained of the ingenuity with which eggs were cooked in religious houses. 'Who can describe', he cries, 'in how many ways the very eggs are tossed and tormented, with what eager care they are turned over and under, made soft and hard, beaten up, fried, roasted, stuffed, now served minced with other things, and now by themselves! The very external appearance of the thing is cared for, so that the eye may be charmed as well as the palate.'

'Fountains Abbey' — George Hodges, 1904

The kitchen windows: on the right is the joining of the vaulting to the refectory wall. The view is from the lay-brothers' dormitory.

The cooks for the week, the abbot's cooks, and the infirmarian were the only monks allowed to enter the kitchen. If there were no fire in the warming-house, the precentor might go in for the purpose of smoothing his wax tablet (the tablet upon which he cut every week the names of the monks who had to take a special part in the services), drying parchment, etc., and the sacristan to get a light for the church or incense. The latter was also permitted to fetch salt on Sundays for the holy water.

'The Ruins of Fountains Abbey'
— Rev. A. W. Oxford, 1910

Rib vaulting in the lay-brothers' refectory (S. end of the lay-brothers' range) 1180-1210. Note the absence of capitals where the ribs spring from the columns. **Compare with page 145.**

But as to the monks themselves, we have a beautifully written and on the whole accurate account in chapter xv. of Newman's 'Life of Stephen Harding,' entitled 'A Day at Citeaux'.

We would gladly have quoted it at great length or even in *extenso*, but the space at our disposal only admits of the following bare abstract. It must be noted first that the year was divided into 'summer' from Easter to Sept. 14, and 'winter,' including the rest of the year. The 'hours' of light were 12, and those of darkness the same, the hours varying from 50 to 70 minutes, as the light was long or short, according to the Roman way of reckoning. The time for rising was about 2 a.m., so that matins, which were shorter in summer, should be over shortly before lauds, which were at day-break. When the sacristan rang the bell, the brethren at once went to their stalls in the choir. Matins lasted for about an hour to an hour and a half, the greater part of the service being chanted by heart to simple Gregorian tones. Between matins and lauds they prayed, read, or meditated in the church or cloister, the interval being short in summer, but long in winter. In summer, the brethren might then go to the dormitory to wash, etc. When day had fully dawned, prime was sung, after which they went to the chapter-house. The chapter opened with the martyrology for the day, after which followed the commemoration of the departed, and on some days a sermon; a portion of St. Benedict's Rule was also read. Then followed open confession of monastic offences and mutual accusation; any monk convicted of grievous offence then receiving the discipline on his knees. Mortal sins were afterwards confessed privately before a priest. Chapter being concluded, the monks went to various kinds of manual labour, in which the *conversi*, or lay-brethren, took a great part. Each monk took his turn to be cook week by week. Again, a monk might be cellarer, infirmarer, master of the novices, porter, etc. The cellarer managed the whole of the 'housekeeping'. All the monks left work when the bell rang for terce, which was at once followed by Mass, after which they again read or meditated. At about 11.30 the bell rang for sext, after which they met in the refectory for the first and chief meal of the day, save on Wednesdays and Fridays out of Paschal time, when they had only one meal, and that after nones. The Cistercian dinner, or breakfast (corresponding to the modern French *déjeuner*), consisted of an allowance (*libra una propensa*) of coarse bread (one-third of which was reserved for supper) and two dishes of vegetables boiled 'without grease'. Their drink was common wine and water, thin beer, or a decoction of herbs. Even fish and eggs were at first excluded, much more any flesh-meat. During meals no conversation was allowed; one of the brethren read aloud from some religious book. The meal over, as is usual in hot climates, and to make up for the shortness of the summer night, they went into the dormitory for an hour's sleep, then rose and washed at the sound of the bell. Nones were said at 2.30, after which they could have a draught of water, or perhaps their daily *hemina* of wine, in the refectory before returning to the afternoon's manual labour, which continued almost till 5.30, when they sang vespers. On returning from their work they had a slight repast, consisting of the remainder of their bread, with fruit, salad, etc.

Before we close with compline, we must note the order of the day in winter, *i.e.* from Sept.14 to Easter.

It was then that they had most time for meditation and prayer between matins and lauds, for lauds being said at dawn came much later in winter than in summer. Prime followed at once, and then came the mass, terce, and chapter, so that they did not begin work till about 9.30 or 10 o'clock. They then worked till nones, after which they broke their fast, *i.e.* between 2.30 and 3.0 p.m. After the meal was over, they walked into the church, two and two, chanting the *Miserere*, and there said grace. Vespers soon followed, apparently before candle-light. In winter no second meal was allowed, only their wine or a draught of water. 'The evening twilight between vespers and compline was the monk's sabbath', devoted to reading and meditation. During Lent they continued working until about 4.0 p.m. not breaking their fast till about 5, and often saying sext and nones in the fields. A longer time was allowed for reading in the morning, and additional mental prayer was enjoined. Throughout the year, the two last events of a Cistercian day were the 'collation' or reading of the collations of Cassian or similar books, and compline. The reading took place in the cloister, and when it was finished they went into the church to sing compline, the last office of the day, at about 7.0 p.m. in winter, and 8.0 in summer. After compline the abbot sprinkled the monks with holy-water as they went out in order. They then pulled the hoods of their cowls over their heads and walked into the dormitory. Such was the Cistercian life in its first fervour, as it was under Stephen and St. Bernard.

Introduction to Cistercian Statutes — J. T. Fowler: 'Yorks. Arch. & Top. Journal', Vol.10 1886

The lay-brothers' day-stairs under which is the entrance to the cellarer's office.

View from the bakehouse ('northern industrial building') with a trough in the foreground: the mounds beyond are unexcavated sites — carpenter's shop, smithy, kilns, barns, etc.

The northern end of the cellarium, 1160-80: note the window later adapted to make

The monastic officers were called 'obedientiaries'; they commanded because they obeyed. Nowhere else could those who had to keep order over large areas find men so fit for their business. For the Church offered a far wider choice of trained servants than the feudal families whose sons were usually taught only to hunt and fight. Through its hierarchy unaccounted men could rise to the proudest posts in Christendom; could become bishops and abbots, justiciars, chancellors and royal ministers.

'The Story of England' — Arthur Bryant, 1953

THE CELLARER.— The cellarer was sometimes called the second father of the house, and he was certainly the Martha of his convent. His duties differed in different orders, but they were always important, and he often took second position to the head. In conjunction with the prelate, he managed the leases, buying and selling of lands, appointing of overseers, and was often away visiting the granges and properties of the convent. The cellarer and the prelate seem to have acted on their own responsibility in the most important matters; and provided they were in agreement, they could do as they pleased with the estates belonging to the house. 'For in matters temporal the cellarer is as it were the prelate's right hand. After the abbot he has the first voice in his own office, and all his servants should obey him as though he spoke with the prelate's lips'. He was responsible for the mills, the malthouse, brew-house and the tolls and carriage of goods. It was his duty to find out whether the men on the granges and their foremen were industrious, or received tips, or stole and sold the property of the house. He had the charge of everything concerning the food, drink and firing and of the granaries. The cellarer's good management meant prosperity, but a house was not always fortunate in this regard. At Bury, Abbot Sampson found that the cellarer was always in debt, and provided a clerk to help him with his accounts, to the indignation of the monks, who considered it an insult for a layman to be placed to watch the work of a regular. This, however, proved unavailing, so for a time he took over the office, saying, 'I have often threatened to take the cellarship into my own hands on account of your defaults and improvidence. I put my own clerk in as a witness, but neither clerk nor monk dares to inform me the real cause of the debts. It is nevertheless said that excess of feasting in the prior's house by the assent of the prior and cellarer, superfluous expenses in the guest-house and the carelessness of the hosteller are the cause of this.' In Abbot Ware's Customary he notes, 'In the hearts of some servants there grows a weariness of divine work and worship and the cellarer had come to regard himself as more at liberty than was fitting.' The temptations were considerable, and to be much abroad was more interesting than the routine of the house.

'The English Abbey' — F. H. Crossley, 1935

The cellarer's office — a rare example of the 12th C.: above, interior; below, exterior.

One of the fishponds in East Applegarths alongside the 14th C. precinct wall.

>*Of wool sold.* Of best wool sold 4 sacks and 15½ stones, £13.5s.3d.
>Of medium wool 24½ stones, 40s.4d.
>Of black wool 1 sack and 2½ stones, 24s.11d.
>Of grey wool (blank)
>Of refuse (blank)
>Of locks 10 stones, 7s.9d.
>Total sacks, 7 sacks and ½ stone.
>Total (£16.8s.6d.) £16.17s.3d.

>*Of sheepskin sold*, 38s.2d.
>Manifest.

>*Herrings and fish.* On 20 salt fish from Wm. Wrampan, 6s.8d.
>On 2 salt fish, 24d.
>To John Weydrall for salt fish and herrings at various times, £3.
>On 5-score salt fish, 42s.10d.
>On salt salmon, 33s.
>On 12 quarters of salt, plus carriage, 43s.2d.
>For the aforementioned salt above, 20s.
>To Wm. Wrampan for 3-score stockfish, 13s.4d.
>Total £11.10s.2d.

Linen cloth.   For the Lord Abbot, on 7 ells of linen cloths, 2s.8d.

On bocasin for the Lord Abbot, 11d.

On 7 ells given to the manor of Kilnsey, 21d.

For the Lord Abbot's buttery, on 20 ells 5s.10d.

For the house of infirm monks, on linen, 8d.

To cushions at Brimham, on linen, 8d.

To the Lord Abbot for various tenants at Baldersby, on 3-score ells, 20s.

Total £1.12s.4d.

Woolen cloth.   (Washing clothes)

To the Lord Abbot, on 2 ell for the bursar, 20d.

To the same, on 2 ells for a scapula, 5s.

To the Lord Abbot and the cellarer, on one dozen albs in blawfront, 20s.9d.

Total £1.7s.5d.

Extract from the Bursar's Books, Fountains Abbey 1457-8: 'Memorials of Fountains Abbey' — Surtees Society, Vol.130 1918

Pro factura serarum per Wm. Smyth, xij*d*.; Pro Curacione equi d'ni Abbatis, ij*s*. vj*d*.; In Cultellis Coquinæ ij*s*. viij*d*.; In Scafis et scutellis de Joh'e Schau, iij*s*. x*d*.; pro perquisicione de vj fodyr plastyr, ij*s*.: In medicinis d'no Abbati per vices, x*s*. iiij*d*.; Cuidam de Dent pro Materia Smertwat, ij*s*.; Pro factura de Carpentwyrke in parte, ix*s*. vj*d*.; Pro Cordis pro plaustris de Haddokstans, viij*d*.; Pro Tinctura vnius scapularis d'ni Abbatis, ij*s*. vj*d*.; In lineo pro flameolis, xxj*d*.: Cuidam de gyllyng pro gatlaw, iiij*d*.; In gallinis emptis d'no Abbati, xj*d*.; In cordis pro carpentarijs, ix*d*.; In suicione linearum d'no Abbati, v*d*. *ob*,; In vna bursa d'no Abbati, x*d*.; In vno pare Caligarum Abbati, xiiij*d*.; In vno pare Cirotecarum vicario de Toplyfe, ix*d*.; In j pare cultellorum Joh'i Marchall, x*d*.; In Smigmate, iiij*d*.; In vna Sera Cameræ Abbatis, vj*d*.; Breuiatori, x*d*.; In papiro, iiij*d*.; In filo Colorato, xix*d*.; Pro ficubus d'no Abbati, vj*d*.; In pergameno d'no Abbati, xj*d*.; In Medicinis d'no Abbati et conuentui pestilenciæ, xij*s*.; Doctori Rievall' in regardo et familo suo, vij*s*. viij*d*.; Mag'ro Marton et familo eiusdem pro Curacione, vij*s*. iiij*d*.; Custodi de Galghay pro carbonibus, v*d*.; Joh'i Hewyke pro labore in inquirendo terras nostras, ij*s*. iiij*d*.: Matildæ Craven pro mensa duorum (puerorum) serratorum, vij*d*.
5. 7. 2 *ob*.

For the making of locks by Wm. Smyth, 12d.; For taking care of the lord Abbot's horse, 2s.6d.; On knives for the kitchen, 2s.8d; On John Shaw's bowls and dishes, 3s.10d.; For the purchase of 6 fodyrs of plaster, 2s.; On medicines for the lord Abbot, from time to time, 10s.4d.; To a man from Dent for Smertwat goods, 2s.; For the making of woodwork, in part, 9s.7d.; For timber, for the carts at Haddockstones, 8d.; For the dying of a scapula belonging to the lord Abbot, 2s.6d.; On linen for flameolae, 21d.; To a man from Gilling, for gatlaw, 4d.; On hens bought for the lord Abbot, 11d.; On wood for the carpenters, 9d.; On the sewing of linen cloths for the lord Abbot, 5½d.; On a purse for the lord Abbot, 10.d; On one pair of shoes for the Abbot, 14d.; On one pair of gloves for the vicar of Topcliffe, 9d.; On one pair of knives for John Marshall, 10d.; On cleaning oil, 4d.; On a lock for the Abbot's chamber, 6d.; To a drawer up of deeds, 10d.; On paper, 4d.; On coloured thread, 19d.; To figs for the lord Abbot, 6d.; On parchment for the lord Abbot, 11d.; On medicines for the lord Abbot and convent in time of pestilence, 12s.; To a doctor from Rievaulx for examination, and his servant, 7s.8d.; To Master Marton and his servant, for care, 7s.4d.; To the warden at Galpay, for coals, 5d.; To John Hewke for work in investigating our lands, 3s.4d.; To Matilda of Craven for food of two (boys) in custody, 7d.

£5. 7s. 2½d.

Extract from the Bursar's Books — Fountains Abbey, 1457-8: 'Memorials of Fountains Abbey', Surtees Society, Vol. 130 1918 (Original entry on left).

The waste grid, measuring 8ft x 6ft in the kitchen of the monks' infirmary. The tunnel beneath it, the most southerly of the four tunnels under the infirmary buildings, is blocked.

Glossary for the preceding 2 pages

Blawfront — term for a white cloth, probably from name of supplier.
flameolæ — a kerchief, or a veil for a chalice or pyx.
gatlaw (or gatla) — gate-law; right-of-way.
fodyr — a measure of weight (nearly a ton).
Smertwat — the word is used later as a family name: what the goods are is uncertain.

Wintry light on the N. face of the lay-brothers' infirmary: their day-stairs are in the foreground.

One of the two drains of the lay-brothers' reredorter, seen from the dormitory.

The abbey required something more efficient than a row of such latrines, so an ingenious type of structure, attached to the monks' house and called its rere-dorter, was designed. Two storeys high, it consisted of a passage running beside which was a stone-lined drain through which was led a stream of water. Above on the first floor was the same passage; beside it, above the slot containing at its base the drain, was provided a row of seats set over this and generally separated by screens. The whole contrivance was an extraordinarily civilized conception. Some rere-dorters were of considerable length, that at Canterbury cathedral priory being over a hundred feet long and seating fifty-five.

Similar buildings had to be attached to the infirmary hall or dorter, and to those portions of the monastery, including the abbot's quarters, in which guests were lodged. The large houses of the lay-brothers in the Cistercian abbeys had to have their own rere-dorter.

It has been computed that Fountains Abbey may have had at one time from five to six hundred monks and lay-brothers in addition to servants and visitors. For the Middle Ages this would represent the population of a small town. The sanitary blocks of such a settlement would need a good water-supply to keep them flushed. The principle of water-borne sewage was, however, fully understood by the monks, who led streams into large tunnels of which the principal, the great drain, formed one of the major factors when starting to lay out an abbey plan on a new site. For a convenient stream had to be at hand, and a route levelled for the great drain so that it would have an even fall and be able to accept branches from all the various rere-dorters as well as the scullery washing-places connected with the kitchens of which there might be several.

Whether any system of sewage disposal existed is not known, but it was realized that the stream should run from the west to east so that the kitchen in its westward position should be able to receive the water when it was reasonably fresh and the main rere-dorter of the monks' house should be the last to use it.

It might be as well to mention here that the great drain of the medieval abbey, long dried out, is the origin of the 'underground passage' of spicy legend.

    'English Abbeys' — Hugh Braun, 1971

The foundations and drain of the monks' reredorter, 1160-80.

The basement of the abbot's house after heavy rain. The three privy shafts in the foreground are in the wall of the early 12th C. reredorter.

The Bursars' book is a folio volume on paper, loose in its vellum cover, and it has suffered greatly from damp, as also, apparently, from the depredations of mice. It has included, when complete, the whole of the receipts and expenses of three years, namely 1456-1459, but several leaves have been lost . . .

After receipts come expenses, first *Firmœ Forinsecœ*, rents or other dues paid by the Abbey to various churches, etc. (£85 14s. 8½d.). Then the expenses of three granges and five tithe barns, servants, or labourers' wages, harvesting, in which work women took great part, hay-making, ploughing, threshing, winnowing, weeding, collecting and carriage of tithe corn and hay, care of cattle, etc., expenses of the *Magister Averiorum* in branding with St. Wilfrid's burning iron or otherwise, etc., driving cattle and sheep, agistment, etc., and of the *Magister Ovium* for care of the sheep, driving them, etc. Much tar was bought; mixed with grease it formed the sheep-salve then in general use. The shepherd carried his tar box about with him, as well as his crook and a pair of shears. Sheep washings and shearings at nine different places are entered separately. Next come entries of wine bought, iron bought, ploughshares, osmunds, shoeing of horses, wainclouts, nails, and a 'pair' of steps. Spices bought, including medicines, 'pepper of ginger', almonds, etc. Herrings and other fish, chiefly salted, including a few salted eels for the Abbot. *Warnesturœ*, including wax, honey, which took the place of sugar in medieval cookery, lamp oil, onions, nut oil, salt fish, raisins, leeks, figs, and salt. *Staurum*, i.e. stock, including boars, sows with little pigs, many horses, mares with foals, etc. Certain sums, *Denarii liberati*, paid to the lord Abbot, to the *monachus coquinœ*, to the *monachus tannariœ*, and to the masters of the cattle, the sheep, of the works generally, and of the lead-mines.

Under *Pannus lineus* we find linen and buckram for the Abbot, and linen for the barber, for the Infirmary, the Refectory, and the Abbot's store-room. Under *Pannus laneus*, a scapular of say for the Abbot, white cloth for the Cistercian habits of the novices, kersey for the Abbot, russet for the servants, an almuce for the Abbot, and much white and black cloth for monastic habits. Swynton mentions cloths called kanyete, meld, albus, and grisius.

Then come *Variœ Expensœ*, extending over several pages. Among these we may note yearly payments of 7s. to the Pope's collector, of 8d. to the Corporation of York for gogyle, £5 to a scholar, 10s. for yeast, also medicines for the lord Abbot, many law expenses, including a brief for the delivery of John Esby, who was imprisoned at the suit of W. Hull, an apostate, shoeing of horses, horse bread for horses of Sir James Strangeways, expenses of the Duke of York at Swanley, paper, parchment, saddles and harness, oat straw for the Abbot's chamber, watching the flocks at Fountains Fell, boots, shoes, and leggings, materials for ink, sea coal, salt, yarn, dyeing, locks, getting plaster, shearing cloth, rakes, etc., to one carrying vessels of bragot, for fowls against Lent, for goat's flesh, for 10 lb. of bronze for a *magna olla*, for seeking stolen oxen, for a 'pair of clavichords,' for little oil-barrels, for green tartaryn for a vestment, for bolting-cloths, to the poor on Maundy Thursday, for mending a silver sprinkler, for a felt hat for the bursar, budge, and other things for the Abbot mentioned above, repairs of a clock, hemp seed, a myrtle [?] for the Abbot, 24 rakes, canvas for woolsacks, a pair of beads for the Abbot, knives and gloves for the servants at Christmas, curing the Abbot's horse, dishes and bowls, soap, charcoal and seacoal, lepes and skeps, razors and sharpening thereof, a deerskin for the Abbot's boots, oat straw for his *camera*, quicksets for hedges, gold thread and silk for vestments, mole-catching and mole-skins, and spreading of mole-hills, a present of 7s. 8d. to a doctor of Rievaulx and his servant, contribution of 10s. to an Oxford student, to a son of John Paslew as a christening present, with expenses, 20s. 9d.; paper for a map of the world, 7 quires for accounts, *pulvis pestilenciœ*, medicines for the brethren, making faggots and hedges, watching a pinfold, *solatia* to friends at Ripon, cabbage and plants, *album ferrum* (tin plates) for lanterns, the Corpus Christi play, special provision for guests, as fresh fish for the Lord William Scrope, swans and other birds for the Earl of Northumberland, for repairing an aumbry at the church and a new lock, collecting

Glossary for this page

Magister Averiorum . . . Master of the cattle
Magister Ovium . . . Master of the sheep
St. Wilfrid's burning iron . . . a branding iron intended to ward off murrain (cattle plague)
osmunds . . . fine quality iron
Wernesturœ . . . miscellaneous stores
monachus coquinœ . . . monk in charge of kitchen
monachus tannerœ . . . monk in charge of tannery
Pannus lineus . . . linen clothing
Pannus laneus . . . woollen clothing
gogyle . . . (unknown)
bragot . . . drink of honey and ale
magna olla . . . great pot
tartaryn . . . rich silk cloth from the East
budge . . . woolly lambskin used as fur
lepes . . . baskets
pulvis pestilenciœ . . . powder against pestilence
solatia . . . help, relief

plants, probably self-sown or other quicksets, required for a hedge by the side of a ditch, a reredos for Crosthwaite. In the changing of a 'saltsaler' a sum of 14s.8d. was paid. Tanners' bark was 'excorticated' at Wheldrake. They paid 20s. to the Vicar of Arncliffe for tithe of Arnclifcote. We find a payment for 3s. 6d. for pitch and rosin *pro navibus*, and the Abbey may have had some ferry-boats or other small vessels of their own on the rivers, though no other mention of such crafts occurs in these accounts or in Swynton's book.

Article on the Bursar's Books by J. F. Fowler: 'Memorials of Fountains Abbey' — Surtees Society, Vol. 130 1918

The most northern of the four tunnels under the refectory end of the lay-brothers' range: unlike the tunnels under the monks' infirmary (page 136) it has no paving.

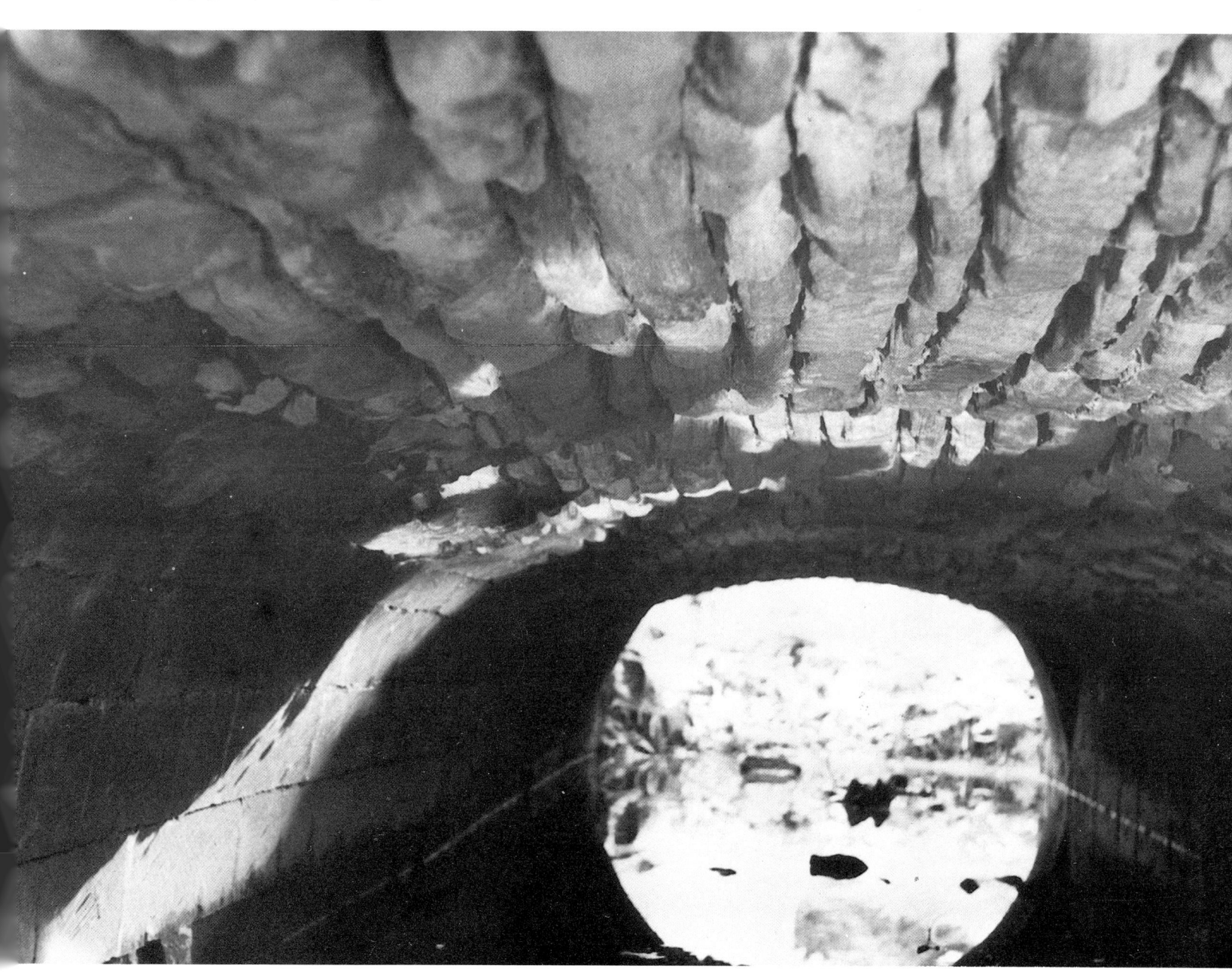

A gateway in the 14th C. precinct wall, on the S. side of the Abbey.

We have noted above that many servants were hired by the monasteries; their number increased as the number of lay-brothers decreased; hence, we find few before 1200; after 1250, their number increased greatly. At Fountains, in the middle of the fifteenth century, there were more than a hundred laborers listed according to their occupations — eight shepherds, nine laborers, five waggoners, five cooks, five foremen, five carpenters, three chamberlains, three foresters, three keepers of pigs, two each of pages, carters, plumbers, wheelwrights, blacksmiths, bakers, workers in the stable, smiths, one each of butler, taylor, yeoman, maker of faggots, barber, washerman, infirmarian, collector of rents, butter maker, lather, as well as several unclassified workers. Those workers received various wages; one got thirteen shillings four pence for making a clock; one got twenty-five shillings nine pence for the same; a carpenter got forty-six shillings eight pence for the year; one man got two shillings eight pence for cleaning a ditch; the blacksmith received six shillings. The washerman got thirteen shillings four pence; the woman who washed the finer cloths, ten shillings; the miller received twenty shillings; a shepherd, four shillings; the pig keeper got thirteen shillings four pence; the stable-worker, six shillings eight pence; the abbot's page received thirteen shillings four pence; the cellarer's page, eighteen shillings.

'A History of the Work of the Cistercians in Yorkshire'
— F. A. Mullin, 1932

Lest he should help himself too freely, the rule of St. Benedict advised that the monk chosen to be cellarer shall not be a great eater (non multum edax).

'The Ruins of Fountains Abbey'
— Rev. A. W. Oxford, 1910

A waste shoot in the cellar of the infirmary chambers leading to the river in the tunnel below: it is also seen on p. 136 — the nearest opening on the right.

A hole for lead piping in the lavatory which took water into a trough, now missing, running along the refectory wall.

The east door of the parlour seen from the infirmary passage. Note the groove in the wall for a pentise or covered way, one of many to be seen around the Abbey offering shelter from the elements. Traces of red paint can still be seen on the plaster around this doorway.

Of the Care of the Ill and the Dying

I commend thee to almighty God, dearest brother,
and to Him whose creature thou art, I commit thee:
as by the intervention of death thou payest the
debt of humanity, so thou returnest to Thy Maker
who made thee from the dust of the earth.

As thy soul issues forth from thy body may the splendid company of angels hasten to meet thee:
may the judge of the council of the apostles come to meet thee:
may the triumphant company of the white-robed martyrs meet thee:
may the lilies of the troop of shining penitents surround thee:
may the joyful chorus of virgins receive thee:
may you be embraced in blessed peace in the bosom of the patriarchs:
may the sight of Christ Jesus appear gentle and joyful to thee:
may He include thee perpetually among His servants.

Ignore all those who shudder in darkness, who cry in flames, who writhe in torments.
May foulest Satan and his attendants depart from thee:
may the train of his angels quake in their coming to thee:
may the vast chaos of eternal night be dispersed.

May Christ free thee from torment, who was crucified for thee:
may Christ free thee from eternal death, who deigned to die for thee:
may Christ the Son of God establish thee for ever among the living in the pleasant green places of His Paradise, and may the True Shepherd acknowledge thee among His sheep:
may he absolve thee from all thy sins, and strongly establish thee at His right hand among His chosen:
may thou see Thy redeemer face to face, and ever present as a servant, may you behold the most manifest Truth with blessed eyes.
Thus appointed to the army of the blessed may you contemplate the divine sweetness, world without end.

Amen.
A prayer from 'Cistercian Ritual and Uses', Paris, 1689

A re-erected pier in the monks' infirmary, 1220-50: the piers once supported arcades.

The Skell in flood passing the great drain and entering the four tunnels over which the infirmary was built. The northern two (left) first pass under the site of the misericord: the southern tunnel (right) is now blocked.

The remains of the arcaded 13th C. passage leading from the cloister to the infirmary. The block of masonry contains a fireplace for a wooden gallery erected above in the 14th C.

The ruins of the house are situated at the south-east angle of the Lady Chapel — a situation dictated, apparently, by a general regulation, but unlikely, in this instance, either to promote cheerfulness or contentment in its inmates. They enjoyed, indeed, a few glimpses of the morning sun; but during the rest of the day were doomed to the sombre shade of the wooded steep which rose far above their roof; and the glorious sunsets down the picturesque Skell — worth the pilgrimage of many a mile to behold — were shut out by the lofty buildings of the convent that filled the bosom of the valley. This particular situation, however, was not obtained without an immense outlay of time and labour; for Skelldale being, at this point, extremely contracted, and the river incapable of diversion, the only resource of the monks was to construct the house *above* the river, and four parallel tunnels or water courses, supporting the foundations, still attest their perseverance and skill.

With an inconsiderable exception, the whole house rested on these tunnels, each arch being ten feet high and as many wide. Their original direction, occasioned by the very precipitous character of the southern bank of the river, is north-east, for the space of about seventy feet; but they then turn full east, and so continue for the space of 197 feet and upwards, for the extremities are broken down. The main walls of the house were arranged with reference to the piers of these tunnels, the influence being particularly visible in the ground plan of the Refectory and adjacent apartments. The sides of these tunnels, based, like some parts of the abbey, on a rock, are of good ashlar work; but their semicircular arches are constructed of coursed rubble, and recently have required much repair, in consequence of the percolation of moisture and the vibration of large trees above. But though the construction of the house above the river might originally be attended with inconvenience, yet the facilities of drainage, ventilation, and cleanliness, were not the least advantages it acquired; and there are, consequently, many apertures and communications from the ground floor to the river, though their purpose has not been uniform, as I will show when I describe the localities where they are found.

'Memorials of Fountains Abbey' — Surtees Society, Vol. 42 1862: an address by J. R. Walbran on the 1851 excavations (he describes what is now known to be the Infirmary).

Hospitals and infirmaries, attached generally to monastic institutions, and intended for the sick, the aged, the orphan and the blind, flourished from the 6th century and developed by the 13th into the semblance of a hospital system, for it was always the duty of the religious to care for the sick even if under some rules and at some times he was debarred from doctoring them.

St. Bernard, the founder of the Cistercian order in the 11th century, not only forbade his monks to practise or become students of medicine but also forbade them when sick to have anything to do with physic. 'To buy drugs, to consult physicians, to take medicines, befits not religion.' They must not use earthly remedies at the risk of salvation. Many of the legends of the saints present the same idea of the incompatibility of religious virtue and the treatment of disease by any means but prayer. On the other hand the huge Carolingian monastery at St. Gall included both a well arranged hospital and a medicinal herb garden.* There was undoubtedly much simple practice of simple medicine . . .

'Sixty Centuries of Health and Physick' — S. G. Blaxland Stubbs & E. W. Bligh, 1931

* From the example of other monasteries, it is thought there was at one time a pharmacy in the infirmary buildings at Fountains, and most probably a herb garden, but there is no actual evidence.

The infirmary was the abode of the sick monks and those who had been professed fifty years. They were in charge of an official called *infirmarius*, who with the help of assistants (*solatium*) acted as their doctor, nurse, and spiritual adviser. In addition to his duties to the sick and aged, the infirmarius four times a year bled the whole community in small batches. In other orders the monks took advantage of this operation to lie up for four days in the infirmary, but this indulgence was not granted to the stricter Cistercians, who were expected to remain in cloister after being bled, though the rule was probably relaxed in later times.

As soon as a monk was ill, the infirmarius fetched from the refectory and dormitory his cup, rations, and bed. From the library he got the sick monk books to read, but had to return them to their places before compline. On Saturdays, if they wished it, he washed their feet and shook out their clothes.*

'The Ruins of Fountains Abbey' — Rev. A. W. Oxford, 1910

* In a footnote, Rev. Oxford indicates that the monks probably shook out a good deal more than dust from their garments.

The most northerly of the four tunnels supporting the infirmary and its buildings, in a dry spell. In the foreground is a double shoot from the cellar, and along the wall are blocked drains and latrine shafts. The tunnels were constructed, as the infirmary, between 1220 and 1250.

Nature's footprints in the infirmary hall.

Among other places on the south side of the abbey, where the natural dip of the valley towards the river particularly favoured the accumulation of rubbish, without offence or suspicion to a careless eye, was one especially, at the south-east angle of the Lady Chapel, occupying a space about 300 ft. long and 180 wide, partly gained by covering the river Skell with four arches or tunnels, which have been immemorially matted over with trees and brushwood... nothing was proposed or ascertained until November, 1848, when the Earl de Grey, who, fortunately for the lovers of antiquity, has recently come into possession of the abbey, directed that a portion of the water-courses or tunnels, which had fallen many years ago, should be repaired. The removal of part of the superincumbent soil being consequently necessary, a fragment of an Early English pavement was discovered, which indicated the important character of the ruined mass, and, in some degree, corroborated the position I had maintained.

After some further trial of the rubbish, which varied in depth from three to six feet, his lordship immediately directed that an excavation of the whole site of the house should be undertaken. During its progress, it soon became evident, that when Proctor had required materials for the erection of Fountains Hall, in the time of James I, the whole of the noble pile had been pulled down as near the foundations as the rubbish accumulated in the

The cellar of the infirmary chambers.

work of destruction would allow. In several places, indeed, the foundation had been reached, and no elevation of masonry suffered to remain that rose above the height of four or five feet. Even the floors were torn up, and nothing was intentionally left on the site except such stones as, from their quality, form, or size, were unfit for further use. As the jambs of the doors and windows, groining ribs, brackets, string courses, and other ornamental portions of the building were, doubtless, best adapted to form grout work in the construction of the new hall, no particular traces of these ravages can be observed there, unless the string course, above the lowest tier of windows, has been removed from some Tudor portion of the older edifice.

For those who can recall his sad eventful history, whose restless ambition thus ravaged hearth and altar alike, it is difficult, while contemplating the wreck of this ancient house, where, for three centuries, so much worth reposed, and benevolence and hospitality were diffused, to forget that a woe hath been denounced against him that 'buildeth his house by iniquity and his chambers by wrong,' or to solve, antipapally, that motto on his purchase-deed of the estate, 'HODIE MIHI, CRAS TIBI.' *

'Memorials of Fountains Abbey' — Surtees Society, Vol. 42 1862: an address by J. R. Walbran on the 1851 excavations (he describes what is now known to be the Infirmary).

* trans: 'My turn today, yours tomorrow'.

Autumn light on the Chapel of the Nine Altars, seen from the cellar of the infirmary chambers: the arches, replacing the E. wall were erected by Mr. Ainslabie in the 18th C.

When from old age or infirmity the monk could no longer take his part with his brethren, he withdrew from the cloister to the infirmary, where his bodily needs were cared for; and he lived dispensed from the exact observance of the rule, but keeping it, or at least being expected to keep it, in the spirit and so far to the letter as his weakness permitted.

The soul of the dying monk was sped on its way with much solemnity. The abbot himself, or in his absence the priest highest in office, administered the last sacraments in the presence of the whole convent, who were summoned to the church for the purpose, and went thence in procession singing psalms by the way, to the place where the sick man lay. When the last moment came, the dying man was laid upon the floor, where ashes had been strewn in the form of a cross. This was a practice not peculiar to Cistercians or even to monks. And even as early as the date of the first written Customs, the Cistercians had so far toned down the harshness of it as to direct that a mat or some straw be laid over the ashes and a quilt over all. The *tabula* or clapper, which was a board hung in the cloister and struck with a mallet, was sounded, and at once, if the monks were at work or in cloister or doing anything which could be left, all hurried to the dying man. If they were in church, some only went, and the others followed when they had finished what they were engaged upon. And so the monk died, with his brethren praying round him.

After death the body was washed in a place

The remains of the infirmary kitchen and chapel.

reserved for that use, and was wrapped in a winding sheet, the convent meanwhile saying an appointed service of psalms and prayers in another place not far away, to which the body was brought when made ready, and the abbot sprinkled it with holy water and censed it, and it was taken to the church with procession and singing. If it were before dinner, Mass for the dead was said, and the body buried that day. But if it were after dinner, the burial was put off until the next day, when Mass could be said; and meanwhile a number of monks were always in the church, keeping up a continual service for the dead. After the Mass the body was solemnly taken to the graveyard at the east end of the church, and there buried. For thirty days a special memory of the deceased was kept in church and in chapter, his name was entered in the book and read out in chapter year by year as his death-day came round, and notice of the death was sent by a special messenger bearing a brief to other houses which were bound by a mutual agreement to do for each others' members as for their own. At every meal a share of the food was set apart in the name of the dead and given to the poor, whose prayers were expected in return.

These memorials after death were very highly valued in the Middle Ages, and it was to obtain a share in them that people living in the world sought to be associated with or, as the phrase then went, to be joined with the *family* of the abbeys. These were the *familiares* of whom mention is made in monastic writings. They took no obligations upon themselves on admission. But generally as benefactors they paid in things temporal for the spiritual benefits which they believed themselves to be receiving. A monk might ask for the prayers of his convent on the death of his father, mother, brother, or sister, and they were to be given, but he might not ask them for others. And each year during the general chapter the dead relations of the brethren of the order were absolved by name by the assembled abbots.

The Cistercian Order — an article by J. T. Micklethwaite: 'Yorkshire Archaeological Journal', 1900

For three days life lingered with slow gasps of breath. So strong was the spirit in his fragile body that, even though his body failed, he was scarce able to give way to death.

In this same time a brother of our society, one of the father's personal attendants, lay sleeping from weariness, and behold! the father, in his infirmity, appeared to him and said, 'Brother, when do you think that I shall depart?' He replied, 'Lord, I know not.' The father, 'My soul, the handmaid of the Lord, will migrate from the earthly home where it has dwelt until now, on the day before the Ides of January.' It happened exactly as the father had foretold to the sleeping brother; for the father left his body on the second day after the brother heard these things from the father.

On the day before he died the Abbot of Fountains and Roger, Abbot of Byland, with nearly all the monks and several of the *conversi*, were with him. A brother was reading the story of Our Lord's Passion, and he was listening, no longer able to speak a word that could be understood. Yet whenever anything was recited of Our Lord's humility or of the faithfulness of the disciples, as he could not speak, he would show his praise and joy in the passage by motions of his hands, sometimes moving his lips in the likeness of a truly spiritual smile. At other places, where Peter denies or the Jews accuse or Pilate assents or the soldier crucifies, he wept and indicated with his fingers the cruelty of the act, and his whole countenance expressed sadness. As the reading proceeded you could see in all joy and grief running together, smiles and tears, the voice of exaltation and the sighs as from one mouth, at one time, the same in all and all in each, on communal procession. To rejoice with the father, to grieve with the father, was an act of piety, just as it is the part of a son to bewail the death of a father and also, as he is still a father, to rejoice with him in his happy release.

'The Life of Ailred of Rievaulx' (abbot of Rievaulx 1146-1166) by Walter Daniel, contemporary of Ailred — (ed. and trans. F. M. Powicke).

THE MISERICORD

The Cistercians adhered strictly to the rule of St. Benedict, which enacted that no flesh meat was to be eaten except by the sick, and only by them during the time of their sickness. No alteration of this rule occurs in the Statutes of 1256, but within the next hundred years, owing to the granting of numerous pittances and the degeneracy of monastic fervour, things had so far changed that the Order was allowed, by a privilege of Pope Benedict XII in 1335, to eat meat in the infirmary and by the invitation of the abbat in his lodging. Further relaxations occurred

Part of the Galilee porch, 1160-80, re-erected from fragments in the 19th C. Such porches were a feature of Cistercian churches and a popular place of burial.

in later years, so that by the middle of the fifteenth century it was the custom to take meat three days in the week, namely upon Sundays, Tuesdays, and Thursdays, excepting in Advent, Septuagesima, Lent, and other seasons of fasting. Though meat was allowed as a permanent luxury, it was not to be partaken in the frater, which necessitated the provision of a special hall for the purpose. As the infirmary was the place where meat was first allowed to be eaten, this hall, or misericord, as it was called, was often in connexion with the infirmary, as at Clairvaux, Fountains, and Beaulieu, and the food was served from the infirmary kitchen. At Kirkstall, Ford, and some other English houses the frater itself was divided by a floor into two fraters, one for use on meat days, and the other on ordinary days, the misericord, which was the lower hall, being served from a new kitchen erected specially for that purpose.

Jervaulx Abbey — St. John Hope & H. Brakespear: 'Yorkshire Archaeological Journal', Vol.15 1911

To all sons of Holy Mother Church, Lambin de Stodlay and Eleanor his wife, greeting. Know that we have chosen sepulture for us in the house of Fountains, and have given our bodies to be buried there whensoever we shall die. We desire therefore that the monks of that house shall be allowed, without hindrance by our heirs or anyone, to receive and convey our bodies to that house when we depart this life; saving, however, the right of our mother-church. And for that devotion and affection (*specialitate*) which we bear towards the said house, we give and confirm to the guesthouse thereof to the use of the guests coming here, a bovate of land with all the appurtenances in the territory of Grantelay, namely that which Adam the miller formerly held from us, and a certain meadow called Halheng in the territory of the same vill, with all the appurtenances, liberties, and easements, as is contained in a certain charter which the monks have thereof. This donation we have made to the said guesthouse under the title (*sub titulo*) of our will, and if anyone should attempt to infringe it, may he have God's curse and ours. That this choice of our sepulture and will may not be infringed by any change of a new will, the present deed is strengthened by the affixing of our seals. *Test.*, Dom. Alan de Aldefeld, John de Traycotes, William de Thorneton, Nicholas his son, William de Merkynfeld, Peter de Merkynfeld, Robert the sergeant (*serviente*) of Stodlay, and others.

'Chartulary of the Cistercian Abbey of Fountains' — Wm. T. Lancaster, 1915

. . . To every monke in Fountaunce Abbey vis. viij*d.*; so that ilkone of thame severally say messe of Requiem for my saule within v dayes they have knaulege of my deth; they specially in thair memento forgyffing me allmaner of bargans had betwene thame and me. To the making of the abbay kirke of Fountaunce x*li* . . .

Sir John Pilkington's will, dated June 28, 1478: 'Yorkshire Archaeological Journal', Vol.29 1929 (C. T. Clay 'Bradley, a grange of Fountains')

A limestone carving (circa 1500) in the Abbey museum. The Virgin Mary is on the right with the Holy Spirit above in the form of a dove. On the left is the Archangel Gabriel, kneeling with a scroll in abbreviated Latin:—
  Ave Maria Gracia
  Plena Dominus Tecum

Hail Mary full of Grace
The Lord is with Thee

Gift By Edulf Of Kilnsey (1174)

Edulf of Kilnsey, to all present and future sons of the holy Church, greeting. May you know that I have given, and confirmed by this present charter, to God and the church of Saint Mary of Fountains and to the monks serving God there, half a carucate of land in Kilnsey as a free and perpetual gift, together with all its appurtenances and easements in wood and plain, in meadow and pasture, in roads and paths and waters and in all places pertaining to the same land, without any reservation for myself and my heirs in perpetuity; discharged, quit and free from all service and custom except for external service which they may make, namely as much as freely and justly pertains to half a carucate of land in Kilnsey, where fourteen carucates make up the fee of a knight. And let it be known that in recompense for this my gift the house of Fountains agrees to receive me, Edulf, as a lay brother and Nicholas my son as a monk, and place my wife in a religious order. Witnessed by the Chapter of Ripon, in the presence of which this agreement was renewed and this charter made. And since I, Edulf, have never owned a seal, by common consent of each party the seal of this chapter is appended to this my charter. Witnessed also by Hugo, abbot of St. Lawrence, Waldef, Stephen and Osbert, vicars of the church of Ripon, William Maciun, Simon de Bedeford, Bernard son of Gamel, Aldred of Ripon, Adam son of Adam son of Meldred. Done at Ripon in the house of William, canon of Bedeford, 15 days after Easter in the year of the Lord's incarnation 1174.

Agreement Between Fountains And William De Rilston (1175)

May it be known to all that this agreement has been made between the monks of Fountains and William de Rilston, namely that the said William has given and confirmed to the aforesaid monks one half carucate of land in Bordley, namely, one bovate at the outset of this gift and another three after his death, or before it if he so wishes. The church of Fountains will receive him when he wishes as a monk or lay brother, if he is healthy enough to be able to be received according to the practice of the Cistercian order, and shall place his wife named Efa in a religious order at a nunnery of her choice within Yorkshire. One of his sons, named Alan, will serve at the house of Fountains in a secular capacity for one or two years, and shall be received as a lay brother should he wish to be received; or, if he has left beforehand, one mark or a horse of the same value shall be given to him; towards looking after his sick son the house of Fountains has already given the said William thirty shillings. Elias his son and heir will confirm this and in exchange will receive his mother's dower in Peter Rilston. If William or Efa should die as lay persons, it will be for them as it would normally be for a monk at the house of Fountains. Witnesses: Simon, priest at Rilston, Ranulf, chaplain at Kirby, Ralph son of Adelin, etc.

Early Yorkshire Charters: 'Yorks. Arch. Soc. Rec. Ser.', Vol. VII

The block of masonry with arches (circa 1180-90) at the extreme N. end of the lay-brothers' range, designed to support the night-stairs above. The entrance to the church is on the left.

The doorway and windows (1160-80) immediately opposite the above arches: before the arches were built, the doorway led from the cellarer's yards, through a parlour into the cloister. Compare the round-headed windows with the later pointed ones (page 111).

Stodeley (circa 1270)

1. GRANT by William son of Walter Creuequer of Stodeley to the gate of Fountains, to the use of the poor gathering there, of a messuage which formerly was Walter's, his father, in the vill of Stodeley, and 3½ acres and a rood of land in the territory of the same vill, lying in these places.

2. GRANT by Philip Veillechen, for the support of the poor of Christ congregating at the gate of Fountains, of a bovate of land in Stodleya Roger, that bovate namely which William son of Mabel (*Mabilie*) formerly held, with the toft and croft belonging to the said bovate. To hold for ever, with the common pasture and other easements, in pure and perpetual alms, free from service, etc. Warranty, and acquittance from everything.

3. QUITCLAIM by Alice formerly wife of Roger de Stodlay, in widowhood, to the monks, for the support of the poor congregating at the gate of Fountains, of a bovate of land with toft and croft and the buildings constructed in it (*in eo*) and all other appurt., in the vill and territory of Stodlay; that bovate namely, toft and croft and buildings, which they have by the gift of Philip Vellechen which (*quam*) she held from the gate of Fountains, in the vill of Stodlay.

'Chartulary of the Cistercian Abbey of Fountains'
— Wm. T. Lancaster, 1915

In 1194, pestilence and famine brought a huge crowd of people to the gate of Fountains. There was no possibility of housing them, but the abbot had wood cut and built huts for them; he appointed stewards to take care of them and priests to look after their spiritual wants. There were so many who died that they had to bury them in pits without funeral rites.

'A History of the Work of the Cistercians in Yorkshire'
— F. A. Mullin, 1932

The fragments left give no idea of the dignity and importance which belonged to the gatehouse and its adjuncts... Special distributions to the poor, varying in amount, were made by appointment of the monastery or of the chapter-general of the order, on eleven occasions annually. The principal dole, on Holy Thursday, consisted of loaves to the value of £6; ten quarters of oat and barley-meal at 6s. the quarter; three barrels of white herrings amounting to 15s.; and ten 'mayses' of red herrings amounting to 60s. Twice in the year a dole of money to the amount of 40s. was made, to every hermit applying 4d., and to every scholar 1d.

'Collectanea Archaeologica'
— British Archaeological Association, 1871

One of the surviving walls of the gatehouse (early 13th C.) near the present entrance to the Abbey: note the precinct wall in the distance.

Large corbels to take a privy in the river wall near the guest houses, indicating one-time extensions: the gatehouse is beyond.

The cloister, showing the stone basin thought to belong to the water system of the Abbey: this is not its original site.

This branch of farming (sheep), which was to become such a source of wealth to the order, became their speciality almost by accident. Wool for clothing had always been a necessity in the village economy, and in the early twelfth century religious and other landowners were already keeping large flocks on down and marshland as a commercial asset. The rising demand of the Flemish cloth industry, however, had not yet been fully met, and in the wolds and moorlands of the north the population was too scanty and conditions too unsettled for any exploitation of the grassland. But it was precisely in these desolate open spaces that the white monks first settled; wool was necessary for their habits and cowls, and it so happened that their sheep were set to graze upon the rolling pastures of Lincolnshire and Yorkshire, which ever since that time have proved among the best in the world for the rearing of noble sheep and the production of the finest fleeces. Sheep farming on a large scale, which had been utterly outside the purview of the small village cultivator, fettered as he was by divided strips, fold-service and labour-dues, was eminently practicable under the grange system of the Cistercian abbeys in the valleys of Lincolnshire, Yorkshire and, later, north Wales, and before the reign of John the annual yield of wool of their fleeces had become one of the assets of the country. In the thirteenth century it developed into a great export trade to Italy and the Netherlands, and for a time the white monks were the most considerable body of producers of wool in England, till gradually the graziers and merchants of Gloucestershire, Somerset, Sussex and East Anglia became supreme. But with these later developments we are not concerned.

An early index of the growth of sheep farming is provided in 1193. In that year a collection was made throughout the country to ransom King Richard. In the case of prelates and churches and the old religious orders this took the form of a requisition of precious metals and jewelry; of this the Cistercians, so far true to their statutes, had little or none, so they were forced to give a year's yield of wool. So keenly was the value of this contribution appreciated that Richard on his way home raised money on the security of the following year's crop (1194), and demanded the wool from the white monks. This would have spelt ruin, and they succeeded in commuting the demand into a sum of money.

'The Monastic Orders in England'
— D. Knowles, 1940

Gift of Simon de Mohaut. (Early 13thC)

Simon de Mohaut, to all present and future sons of the Holy Church, greeting. May you know that I have given, ceded and confirmed by this present charter, to God and the monks of the church of Blessed Mary of Fountains, for the use of poor seculars lying in the infirmary of Christ, for the safety of my soul and that of all my ancestors and heirs, together with my body to be buried there, John son of Godwin of West Morton my bondsman, with all his issue and that bovate of land, with toft and croft, which he has held in the vill with all its appurtenances, freedoms and easements within and without the vill. And moreover I have given them sufficient pasture for 200 sheep and four roods of land in length, one and a half in breadth, of the croft which Gilbert the cook once held at the top of the same vill to the north, namely in the furthest part of the said croft to the west, to make a sheepfold, together with one acre of land lying immediately alongside the said croft next to the moor, with freedom of exit and entrance and all other easements everywhere within the common land belonging to the vill, without any reservation for myself or my heirs. All these things I have given them to have and to hold of myself and my heirs as a clear and perpetual gift discharged, free and quit of all service and secular demand or charge and anything pertaining to the land. And I and my heirs will warrant all the aforementioned to the aforesaid monks for the use of the said poor, and will defend it against all in perpetuity; if any of my heirs shall presume to obstruct this my gift in any way or to withdraw it from the aforesaid and convert it to other uses, let him know that he has incurred the anger of God and my curse, and because of this he will be in fear of divine vengeance upon him unless he repents. Witnessed by the following: William of Styveton, Richard Gramar, Nicholas de Barkeston, Matthew de Hagnewrth, John de Hakkewrth, Robert de Greenhill, Robert the villein, and others.

Early Yorkshire Charters: 'Yks. Arch. Soc. Rec. Ser.', Vol. VII.

Kilnsey Old Hall, 17th C. built on the site of the original Kilnsey grange.

From the foot of Penigent to the boundaries of St. Wilfrid of Ripon, the estates of this wealthy house (Fountains) stretched without interruption. Fountains Fell still retains the name of its ancient possessors; all the high pastures from thence to Kilnsey were ranged by their flocks and herds; Kilnsey and Coniston were their property . . .

Kilnsey was the place to which the immense flock of this abbey were driven from the surrounding hills for their annual shearing; a scene of primitive festivity to which the imagination delights on recurring.

The bleatings of the sheep, the echoes of the overhanging rocks, the picturesque habits of the monks, the uncouth dress, long beards and cheerful countenance of the shepherds, the bustle of the morning and the good cheer of the evening, would altogether form a picture and a concert to which nothing in modern appearances or living manners can be supposed to form any parallel.

'The Deanery of Craven' — T. D. Whitaker, 1878

On the borders of Pen-y-ghent and Fountains Fell.

Bewerley Chapel, now restored and open as a chapel for prayer.

From De Burun it (the Manor of Bewerley) passed in a very short time to the family of Mowbray, Earls of Northumberland, and was by Roger, first baron of that name, given to the Abbot and Convent of St. Mary, of Fountains. The worldly wisdom of the monks was never more prominently displayed than in the care they took to make good their title to the lands thus bestowed on them; they obtained charter after charter renewing or confirming they respective grants, not only from the chief lords of the fee, but from every one who could be supposed to have any claim or interest therein. The grants of Mowbray were confirmed not only by the King, but also by the Archbishop, and Dean and Chapter of York, by Alice de Grante, wife of Roger de Mowbray, and afterwards by the successive barons De Mowbray, down to Thomas, who died an exile at Venice in the year 1400. These grants included not merely the surface soil, but also all mines of lead, iron, metals, and minerals beneath the surface. By one charter, Roger de Mowbray gave to the Abbot and Convent part of the Forest of Nidderdale, west of the river Nidd, with the use of the customary roads, and a new one thirty feet in width. This gift was confirmed by King Henry II . . . Another charter confirmed to them the ownership of all mines of iron, lead, and other metals and minerals in the Forest of Nidderdale.

'Nidderdale' — William Grange, 1869

At Brimham there were two monastic properties within half a mile of each other. Brimham Grange (now known as Brimham Hall) was a dairying grange, carrying a herd of forty cows. Brimham Park (now known as Brimham Lodge) was used by the abbots as a country residence and hunting lodge, and for this reason remained in the direct control of the abbey. The keeper of the Park was given a house, and pasture for

The motto of abbot Huby on the east wall of Bewerley grange chapel — (Bewerley by Pateley Bridge).

a horse, three cows, and thirty sheep, in return for supervising the cattle, meadows, and fences, but he had no produce or stock to deliver.

None of the monastic farm buildings has survived intact, although fragments of earlier structures were incorporated when several of the granges were rebuilt in the late seventeenth century. Bewerley Chapel, which dates from the time of Marmaduke Huby, abbot from 1494 to 1526, still stands; and a wall of the grange chapel at Ramsgill survives in the modern churchyard. No trace remains of the chapel at Bouthwaite, but at Brimham Hall the stones of the former chapel can be seen in the walls of the fields and buildings, where cattle rub against fragments of Abbot Huby's motto 'Soli Deo Honor et Gloria' (Honour and Glory to God Alone), and of other Latin inscriptions.

'A History of Nidderdale' — ed. Bernard Jennings, 1967

The grange of the monks at Bewerley at that time (the Dissolution) was valued at £16 16s. 8d. per annum. The chapel built by them yet exists . . . plain and humble, yet bearing unmistakable evidence of its use, and also of its builders; the motto in large old English letters,

Soli Deo honor et gloria

And the huge M.M. of Marmaduke Huby, abbot of Fountains, from 1495 to 1526, are yet conspicuous on the walls; the motto is on the east end, and the initials on the east, north, and south sides. It is a low building; the windows are of three lights each under a square label moulding. The entrance is through an elegant little porch on the south. The bell turret yet remains at the east end. The walls are prettily overgrown with ivy, moss, and ferns.

'Nidderdale' — William Grange, 1869

In 1276, the abbot of Fountains sold sixty-two sacks of wool to Florentine merchants to be delivered in installments for the next four years at Clifton (on the Ouse, near York) prepared and weighed at the monks' expense. For this they were paid in advance the same sum of 697½ marks, or about five pence per pound . . . (*see opposite page*).

The great variance in the figures connected with the Cistercian wool growing would indicate that there were many fluctuations of fortune connected with it. A very profitable year might easily be followed by a disastrous year. The number of times that each monastery was in debt, together with the size of those debts, seems to indicate that broad acres and large flocks, intermittent as the latter may have been, did not guarantee a large stabilized income. Many of the Yorkshire houses were often in debt, and at times for rather large sums. Meaux seems to have been especially unfortunate in this regard. Debts caused a disperal of the monks in 1160, and again in 1196 . . . Fountains was encumbered for £233 in 1278, and twelve years later, for £6373; the financial condition of the house was so bad at this time that it was placed in the hands of the king.

In 1251 a great drought reduced the hay crops by half and also caused a great loss of live stock. Just a century later, in 1353, there is a record of the failure of all crops, and food had to be imported. There were few years during the last half of the reign of Edward III (1352-1377) when the wool trade was not interfered with by pestilence or parliament . . . It is impossible to discover to what extent the production and exportation of wool was affected by the plague because there are no custom returns for the years when the customs were farmed. The 35,596 sacks exported 1350-51 were over the average of the time, 30,000 sacks; after this there were sharp decreases and increases. Sheep raising was open to many hazards on account of severe losses in the flocks. In one instance, an owner of about 1200 sheep, kept in eight different places, reported losses of 308 in one year, 242 another, 300 a third, and 34 the fourth year from the 'rot'. The scab appeared in 1280 and from that time on all flocks had to be treated with tar.

from 'A History of the Work of the Cistercians in Yorkshire'
— F. A. Mullin, 1932

The following deed, entered into by the Abbot and Convent on this occasion, is similar to other instruments drawn up in like cases by the wary money-lenders of the 13th century.

'To all who shall see these present letters. Fr. D., called Abbot of Fountains, and the Convent of the Cistercian Order of that place, in the diocese of York, greeting in the Lord.

'KNOW ye that we have sold and granted to Dunelm Fonte and Bernard Thedald, buying and receiving as well for themselves as for Theclan Thedald, brother of the said Bernard, and their other partners, citizens and merchants of Florence, sixty-two sacks of wool, of the various flocks of our monastery, without clack, and lok, gode and card, or hairy, refuse fleece; and without the skin. Which wool we promise prepared and weighed out at our proper expense and cost, and bind ourselves to deliver it by lawful stipulation within the terms written, — viz. on the fifteenth day after the nativity of St. John the Baptist, AD 1277, seventeen sacks; — also on the same day in AD 1278, seventeen sacks; and also fourteen sacks, AD 1279; and fourteen other sacks on the said fifteenth day, AD 1280, in every such year at Clifton, to the aforesaid merchants, or one of them, or to a trusty deputy of theirs, bringing these letters, without further delay. For which sixty-two sacks, to be given and delivered up in the place and at the times now mentioned, the said merchants will have paid to us before our hands at London, six hundred and ninety marks and a half, good, new, and lawful monies, — thirteen shillings and four pence computed for each mark. Of which money, in our name and in that of our monastery, we call ourselves well and truly quit and satisfied, renouncing wholly every exception touching the non-payment or non-delivery of the money to us. But if the said wool, as was said, shall not have been wholly delivered and given up to the said merchants, in the place and at the times aforesaid then we promise to them, and are bound by the aforesaid agreement, to refund, and render back, and restore to the same merchants, or one of them, or a trusty deputy of theirs, all expenses and losses and interest which the said merchants have paid, or incurred, for defect of rendering up and delivery or assignment of the said wool ………………………………………………………
………………………………………………………

In witness of which we have set our seal to these present letters. Given at London on the eve of the feast of St. Luke the Evangelist (Oct 17) AD 1276.'

Clack — The tar-mark of the fleece. Lok, Lock — the short cuttings. Gode — 'Gallis erat ovis vetula.' — The fleece of an aged ewe appears to be meant. Card — Matted wool.

'Delineations of Fountains Abbey'
— J. & H. S. Storer (circa 1830)

Much uncertainty exists as to the use of this room. The drawbar of the doorway and the fastenings of the passage door could only be used by someone inside, and though of course the swinging bar may be of later date than the Suppression, when the courts of the Liberty of Fountains were held here, the drawbar was provided for from the first. The absence of a garderobe shews that it can hardly have been a living or sleeping room of one of the officers of the abbey. Possibly, being fireproof, this was the muniment room of the abbey, for which it is admirably suited, and the door fastenings may have been to keep intruders out while important documents were being examined, though this seems an overcautious provision.

'Fountains Abbey' — St. John Hope:
Yorks. Arch. Journal, Vol.15 1898

Its size is not surprising when it is remembered that in addition to the convent's archives (and Fountains had more than 3500 title deeds to its extensive lands) it probably housed the deeds and treasure of local secular lords, for the great abbeys often acted as safe deposits for these.

The Fountains Abbey Guide Book
— R. Gilyard-Beer, 1970

The warming house, S. side, with muniment room above: the railings indicate the head of the day-stairs leading to dormitory (right) and muniment room.

Letter of Archbishop Roman (1294)

To the monks of Clairvaux, of the Cistercian order, visitors assigned to England, on the state of the house of Fountains.

Since the noble monastery of Fountains, of the said order, of our diocese, has in these days (we are sad to relate) fallen to such poverty that as a result of its woeful ruin — of which the whole kingdom speaks, as we quite clearly explained to the saintly man, our dearest friend the Lord Abbot of Citeaux, when we were abroad — it has (alas) become a laughing-stock to everyone; and no wonder, since because of some people who behave with inward pride and outward compassion the worship of God is belittled in the very house which our predecessors as Archbishops of York founded and which they themselves and other nobles of the kingdom most generously endowed with donations of land, property and possessions, the patrimony of Christ is eaten away, alms embezzled, charity despised, the Rule neglected, devotion rejected, the wickedness spreads of some who fire the tinder of jealousy amongst them by conspiracies and alliance, and sincere enthusiasts of the Order are driven out and taken to somewhere outside, to the said monastery's loss. We, who, by reasons of its foundation and the position of patron which we are known to hold in the house, suffer equally from its misfortune and its innermost despair, ask as friends your friendship and discretion regarding the reform of the said house, which we desire, so that you may turn eyes of compassion on its wretched state and the abovementioned factions and see that a diligent investigation and enquiry is made by yourselves and your officers; and those whom you find guilty may you compel to spend time in the Order elsewhere until the house is relieved of the burden which weighs it down, and recall those sent away through the conspiracies of the envious, so that the condition of the house may change for the better by your assent, which, if God is on our side, will happen given your fairly balanced weighing of our statements. Farewell.

'Memorials of Fountain Abbey' — Surtees Society, 1876

muniment room windows seen from the treasury: the warming house chimney is on the left.

Fountains abbey also was a Lake District proprietor. It acquired from Alice II de Rumelli by various transactions beginning about 1195, the church, vill and mill of Crosthwaite, and Hestholme (Derwent Island) and Watendlath and Langstrath. One would hardly expect bits of this land to be so valuable as they turned out to be under the management of Cistercian monks, who were nothing if not great farmers. The two abbeys, Furness and Fountains, made an agreement in 1211 fixing their borders more exactly, and Stonethwaite in Borrowdale was left on the Fountains side of the line. Later on, when the dairy farm there had become prosperous, somebody at Furness abbey regretted that it had gone to Fountains, and started the idea that the agreement had been unfairly influenced by their brother Nicholas, who had been a Fountains monk. The dispute was referred first to other Cistercian abbots; then it was taken to the Chapter General of the Order, who decided for Furness in 1302, but Fountains would not accept the decision. The abbot of Cîteaux appointed the abbot of Holme Cultram and another, not in this district, to settle the case, but they differed. In 1303 the bishop of Carlisle wrote to the abbot of

The east guest house beautified by snow.

Cîteaux protesting against breaking the agreement of 1211; but next year the referees came to a decision in favour of Furness. Then, the custodian of Cockermouth Castle wrote to the Barons of the Exchequer that a judgement respecting ownership of land had been given without consulting the king, which of course was illegal; and so the king took the little vaccary of Stonethwaite into his own hands. Fountains was equal to the emergency and offered the king forty shillings to have that pasture — and got it.

'Lake District History'
— W. G. Collingwood, 1928

Early summer. Light on the Abbey.

The west face in morning mist.

fall in March.

In 1346 an agreement was made between the Chapter of Ripon, and the abbot and convent of Fountains respecting the chapel of St. Michael del Monte, situate on the beautiful mount now called How Hill, about a mile south of the abbey. This chapel was doubtless built by the brethren on this their first acquired and favourite estate, and was probably attended by the inhabitants of Markington, and the laymen resident at the granges of Morker and Haddockstones, which were near adjoining. Being situate within the parish of Ripon, the Chapter claimed authority over it, and the matter was settled by the latter allowing the monks to celebrate divine service in the said chapel on St. Michael's day, or on other days of the year, and receive all oblations and obventions whatsoever coming to the said chapel; on condition that they should not introduce use, or administer the sacraments, or any other thing to cause loss or prejudice to the said church of Ripon; and for this privilege the abbot and convent agreed to pay to the church of Ripon the sum of two shillings and sixpence yearly on the feast of the exaltation of the Holy Cross.

'Annals of a Yorkshire Abbey' — William Grange, 1896

A magnificent view over the plain of York is obtained from *How Hill*, about ¾m SW of Fountains Abbey. There was a chapel of St. Michael on its summit, but the tower now seen there was built by Mr Aislabie in 1778. A stone built into the wall bears the initials of Abbot Huby, with his motto. The hill was anciently called 'Herleshow', either, suggests Mr Walbran, as the place where the Saxon Earl of the county held his court, or from some early proprietor named 'Herled'.

Murray's 'Guide for Travellers in Yorkshire', 1882

The Chapel of St. Michael, How Hill.

Winter light over the refectory.

Thunder clouds over the chapter house.

Licence to Convert Granges to Secular Use (1363).

Greetings from the abbots of Rievaulx and Byland. A letter has been received from the abbot of Cîteaux, the substance of which follows:

'We, brother John, abbot of Cîteaux, make known to all that in the year of Our Lord 1363 at Viviers, in our General Chapter, a decision was taken in the following terms. The General Chapter granted a request from the Abbot and Convent of Fountains, in England, to the effect that, since before the wars between the Scots and the English they possessed many granges which are now lost, burnt and reduced virtually to nothing and cannot be rebuilt, they should be empowered to transfer them to laymen on payment of annual rent and create vills there; also that the abbots of Rievaulx and Byland should be assigned to this matter as commissaries, who should act in the aforementioned business as would appear beneficial to the house of Fountains. As witness of this we have seen fit to append our counterseal. Dated in the abovementioned year and place, on the day of the Blessed Lambert, bishop and martyr.'

After the presentation of this letter and our receipt of it, we were informed in greater detail that the abbot and convent had and still have granges (namely Aldborough, Slenyngford, Sutton, Couton, Cayton, Bramley, Bradley, Kilnsey and Thorp) attached to their monastery which, through the hostile raids of the Scots, the misfortunes of war, the plagues of mortality and bad weather long persisting in those parts, and other chance occurrences, were and are largely ruined in their buildings; their lands, once fertile and bountiful, are reduced almost to barrenness, because the abbot and convent have not the capacity to rebuild the aforementioned buildings, so ruined and collapsed, or to cultivate the lands for their benefit, nor does it appear that they will be able to gather from them in future. So they urgently pressed their plea with us, since we had duly considered and carefully attended to previous and different misfortunes and needs of themselves and their aforementioned monastery, that they should be allowed to convert and reduce the aforesaid granges into vills, and should be able to transfer them to laymen for an annual rent, and that we should deal with these arrangements by the authority granted to us in this matter. We, therefore, abbots of Rievaulx and Byland, the aforesaid commissaries, wishing to investigate the information given to us by the abbot and convent of Fountains, enquired painstakingly and diligently into the truth of the evidence and the request.

The truth and reasonableness of the request being confirmed by the testimony of good witnesses, a licence is duly granted. Names of the Notary and the Abbots, together with those of other witnesses to the document, are given.

'Memorials of Fountains Abbey' — Surtees Society, 1876

[AD 1391-1431; possibly 1449-52].

To their — — — founder the Archbishop of York, Primate and Chancellor of England.

— — — the abbot and convent of Founteyns of your foundation that whereas John de Preston of Malgham and William de Preston of Otirburne in Craven the 10th day of December last with force and arms came to their abbey in the hour of vespers and there in the cloister and the sanctuary made great affray and assault on the monks and the servants there with their swords, spears and other weapons, wishing to have killed those whom they found there present, and then they lying in wait for the abbot, his fellow-monks and servants in the parts of Craven took a monk and officer of the abbey Dan John de Preston and would have killed him unless he made fine with them of two marks which they took from him; and also they are still lying in wait against the abbot and convent and their servants, and menace them with death to their persons and their cattle to the very great damage of your Chaplains and against the peace of our lord the King; wherefore your Chaplains beseech humbly your very reverend Paternity that it please you to send for the wrongdoers and their helpers by brief of *Quibusdam certis de causis** or other at your pleasure to have them before you and the Council of our lord the King in his Chancery and have them chastised according to your very high discretion so that your Chaplains and their servants may be in peace and other such wrongdoers be chastised by their example.

* certain established charges.

[XIV and XV Cent.]

To the right gracious Lord Chancellor of England.

Beseecheth full humbly your devout orator the abbot of Founteyns that whereas John Tenant of Netherhesilden, John Man, late of Thorpe under Wod, Rogar Tenaunt of Eveston, William Felebrig otherwise called William Wade of York, Thomas Paliser of Sandehoton and James Osbaldeston, Esquire, gathered unto them many riotous and misgoverned people arrayed in manner of war, the tenants and servants of the abbot, that is to say his menial servants, his bailiffs, Receivers, and shepherds being on the field keeping his sheep, assaulted them, beat them, wounded them, and so from day to day threatened them to slay that they dare not abide in his service for dread of death, and if so be that any action be taken against them at the common law they remove and go into dales and fells so that there may be no common law executed against them, to the great hurt and prejudice of your orator but if [i.e. unless] he be otherwise remedied by your grace.

[*plea for writs* sub pena *to each of the misdoers*].
Pledges: William Gayng of London
        Robert Babyngton of Con-[*torn*]

Monastic Chancery Proceedings: 'Yorks. Arch. Soc.', Vol. 88 1934

The rebus of Abbot John Darnton on a corbel above the great west window (taken from scaffolding during restoration). John *is represented in the eagle of St. John, the word* dern, *now almost obliterated was on the left part of the scroll, and* ton *is the tun or cask held by the eagle. The eagle also holds a crozier, and the inscription to the right reads 1494. The whole corbel supports a statue (now headless) of the Virgin Mary.*

Meaux Abbey

[*Latin*]

[*c.* AD 1404]

To ——— the Lord Bishop of Exeter, Chancellor of England.

Beseecheth humbly the General Chapter of the Cistercian Order whereas Robert de Burley, Abbot of the monastery of Fountains, and Thomas de Burton, pretended abbot of the monastery of Melsa of the same Cistercian Order in Yorkshire, in wanton defence of the excesses and errors which Brother Robert, abbot of Fountains, committed concerning the vicious promotion of Thomas to abbot of Meaux contumaciously opposed themselves and wilfully made insurrection with a great band of secular persons in contempt of and against the peace of our lord the King and in scorn of their Order and of religion, with force of arms and with gates shut and with ambushes set making a fortress of the Abbey of Meaux did wantonly resist and drive away the abbot of the monastery of Roche ['Rupe'], the Visitor and reformer of their monastery of the Cistercian Order in the province of York, and the abbot of Gerondon associated with him threatened the abbots of Roche and of Gerondon and their servants with mutilation and slaughter, and also they put down with force and arms within their monastery the prior, sub-prior and convent of the Abbey of Meaux because they wished to obey the Reformer according to the statutes of their Order and to resist these forfeits and abuses; and also the abbots of Fountains and of Meaux received a certain Sigismund a foreign monk coming into England with a certain pretended power to cite the abbots of

The rebus of Abbot John Darnton on the south end of the Chapel of the Nine Altars — the carving was intended to mend a fracture in the stonework. The angel has dern *on his breast, and the eagle and tun are as opposite. An inscription translated reads O ye wells, bless ye the Lord.*

the Order, lieges of our lord the King, to a certain pretended General Chapter outside the kingdom of England, and did send the said monk out of the kingdom with many gifts of gold and silver and other jewels, against the gracious concession of our most holy Father the Pope for the protection and special inhibition of our King; wherefore may it please the Venerable Father the Lord Chancellor to grant special briefs to the Sheriff of Yorkshire to make the abbots of Fountains and of Meaux to come with their accomplices before you and the Council of our lord the King to answer wherefore they have presumed in manner as aforesaid; may it please also the Venerable Father to renew in another form a certain especial protection and inhibition of our lord the King elsewhere graciously conceded to the abbots of Boxley, Stretford and Griis delivered here and to grant a special brief to the Sheriff of Yorkshire that he may make proclamation of this protection and inhibition in the City of York, in Beverley and Rypon and in all other markets within the County lest the contumacious abbots of Fountains and Meaux or other lieges of our lord the King may assume the rash and daring boldness of making insurrection against the Visitor and reformer and other Inquisitors and Judges of their Order aforesaid. In the way of charity.

The names of those secular persons who have made insurrection with the abbots of Fountains and Meaux.

    John Rednes
    William Constable
    Armandus Veel   of Holderness
    John de Towton
    John Taleor
    Roger Mawdit of Fountains, and many others.

Monastic Chancery Proceedings: 'Yorks. Arch. Soc. Rec. Ser.', Vol.88 1934

Abbey Precincts

20 February 3 Henry VIII [1512]. Lease [*in Latin*] by Abbot Marmaduke and the Convent of Fountains to Robert Dauson and Ellen his wife (by their unanimous agreement) of a house or hospice outside the west gates of the monastery, newly-built, a small close adjacent called Ryebanks, a close called Gest Stabyll Inge, a portion of the closes of Skell Bankes and Skell Homes . . . the abbot and convent grant that Robert and Ellen, for the term of Ellen's life, are to receive week by week at the monastery's larder all intestines called *lez ishewes* of all the cattle (*averia*) and sheep killed for the use of the monastery, except cattle killed and assigned to the larders around Christmas, paying every year for the same on their account according to the value and price customary before, namely 3*d* for every beast (*averium*) and 16*d* for every score (*vigenarius*) of sheep. Robert grants by these presents that he will faithfully serve the abbot and his successors, especially on festival and solemn days within the monastery, and also in all suitable and lawful foreign business placed on him by them at their expense, and also that he will diligently attend and fulfil the office of porter at the west gates, and keep or cause them to be closed at night at fitting and convenient hours at the time of fairs (*nundine*) and other occasions, and in addition that he will keep all the wood and underwood growing within his tenements (*tenure*) and will not lop (*loppo*) any timber for the pasturing of cattle in destruction of the same, and will not make or permit any waste to be made. He will show and present all trepasses and damage found by him there before the steward and officials at the court of Aldefeld. For faithfully executing and fulfilling the which services and offices, Robert and Ellen will have 13*s* 4*d* in reward allowed to them in their account from the sum of 53*s* 4*d* levied in farm for the said house or hospice. In addition Ellen agrees that she will wash or cause to be washed whenever necessary all the linen cloths (*linthiamina*) in any way pertaining to the buttery (*aula promptuarium*), common hospice and the lord abbot's chamber, without deliberate injury or tearing of them. She and an honest washerwoman (*lota*), serving the monastery with the same tasks, of her good and gratuitous diligence will carefully and fully repair and will mend or cause to be mended tears in the same when they have been found, for the which service, well and diligently performed, Ellen will have 13*s* 4*d* in money allowed to her every year on her account from the rent for the house or hospice. She will also receive annually twenty waggon-loads of fuel (*plaustrate focalium*), of the provision of the convent, brought and allowed her by the lord's cart (*cariagia*), for burning in the said service. Lastly the abbot and convent (by their unanimous agreement and benevolent disposition) grant Robert and Ellen by these presents that they will receive, during Ellen's life, for their livery every week seven loaves of the better [bread] and seven of the second at the monastery's bakehouse, six gallons of the better service and six of the second, and in every day's allowance of food (*dieta*) of the convent, one dish (*ferculum*), both of meat and fish, as much as is served to two monks, to be received at the abbot's kitchen. If Ellen dies before Robert, he is to receive exactly half the said livery. If the rent remains unpaid for three months, besides the allowances allowed in the same, the abbot and convent have the right to distrain for the rent and arrears (if there are any), and if it is one year overdue, or if Robert and Ellen make or endeavour to make wilful waste in the woods, to the grave damage of the monastery, the abbot and convent can re-enter and relet at their pleasure, this lease notwithstanding. Robert and Ellen agree by these presents to maintain all the houses and buildings now constructed or afterwards built on the tenement, and all ditches, hedges, drains and other defences pertaining to the tenements, except necessary repairs to the house or hospice, which [will be] reserved to the abbot and convent's charge, and large timber, which will be delivered and assigned to them as necessary for their other repairs. In addition the abbot grants of his benevolence to Robert and Ellen that he will build or cause to be built at his own cost, as fitly as he is able, an appropriate and convenient stable near the house or hospice to the use of themselves and their guests (*hospites*), the which guests Robert agrees to these presents to receive and care for diligently and humanely in everything, both in word and deed, and to treat them courteously and kindly in the accounts of their expenses, as far as he is able, without damage to the honour of the monastery or of himself. Sealed interchangeably, the abbot and convent affixing their common seal.

Fountains Abbey Lease Book — ed. D. Michelmore: 'Yorks. Arch. Soc. Rec. Ser.', Vol.140 1981

The Abbey seen from the Studley Royal grounds.

Darnton's east window (between 1483 and 1493) which replaced three lancets and a wheel window above.

Part of the north window of Huby's tower, started circa 1495.

THE TOWER

A perfect, chaste, and beautiful specimen of perpendicular architecture, the most recent of all the buildings of the monastery; the work of Abbot Marmaduke Huby (1495-1526), and which with trifling damage to the battlement, and the loss of the tracery of one window, is yet as complete as when it came from the builder's hands; the walls being remarkable fresh, and the ornamental details of mouldings, niches, canopies, and pinnacles on the flanking buttresses nearly perfect. It rises in four stories to the height of 168 feet, with an internal area at the base of 25 feet square. Above the window of the first story on the west side is the sculptured figure of an angel standing on the canopy of a vacant niche, holding a shield on which is carved a mitre and croiser and the letters M. H. In another niche over a window on the north side is a crowned female figure holding a palm branch in her right, and a book in her left hand;* and on the southern side above the ridge of the transept, is a gowned effigy holding a croiser in his right, and a book in his left, probably intended for that of Huby himself.† No verbal description can do justice to the details of this splendid fabric. Fillets run round the four sides

Huby's tower, made of limestone: note the sandstone quarry from which the 12th and 13th C. buildings were made.

above and below the belfry windows, on which are raised inscriptions in bold black letter, intermixed with shields of arms; the upper are so weather worn as to be illegible; the lower consist of quotations from the offices of the church; the shields are chiefly those of the abbey — three horse shoes — and a maunch, the bearing of the Nortons, of Norton Conyers, who must have been liberal contributors towards the erection of the work. It is believed that the remains of Marmaduke Huby, the builder, found their last resting place at the base of the magnificent pile which his skill and energy had erected — and never had mortal man more fitting sepulchre.

* now known to be St. Catherine
† more possibly St. Benedict or St. Bernard

'Annals of a Yorkshire Abbey' — William Grange, 1896

So it was with the monastic order of Cistercians; it began with a fair promise, and really did great and good work in a world of semi-barbarism. The prodigal munificence of benefactors was one of the great causes of its ruin. Had its members continued in that happy state spoken of by Solomon, with neither riches nor poverty, they might have fulfilled their mission. Little did the kind and charitable, who bestowed lands upon them in perpetual alms, think that by no means they were working the ruin of those they patronised . . . When the Cistercian monks were poor they kept the rule in its purity; laxity of discipline and worldly pomp grew upon them as their wealth increased. Their plain and meagre diet gave place to one more profuse and luxurious; their vegetables were seasoned with butter and oil, and flesh meat was on pretence of special dispensation from the pope; they also introduced another meal in the day, and were not afraid of indulgence in wine. Their churches at first were distinguished by their naked plainness and stern simplicity; and their dresses were of the same plain, simple, and inexpensive kind; no ornaments of silk of gold were allowed on the robes of the monks or abbots. In 1152, it was first permitted for monks of this order to wear copes of silk during the ceremony of their benediction, but at no other time. In 1257, permission was given to the abbots to wear a cope on all days when they used the pastoral staff, and on all days when white was the colour of the day. In 1157 monks were forbidden to wear copes or dalmatics, even when assisting a bishop at high mass in a church of the order, but in 1257 they were permitted to wear dalmatics and tunicles when simply assisting their abbot; and in 1226 chasubles of silk were fully allowed, if they were not bought by the abbey, but bestowed on it as gifts.

The insides of their churches also became changed by degrees; gilded crosses were allowed in 1157, if not of large size; in 1256 the altars were allowed — on grand festival days — to be dressed with frontlets of pure silk. Sculptured ornaments and costly marbles adorned the fabric, and majestic towers appeared instead of the simple wooden belfrey allowed by the first constitutions. In 1489 the abbot of Clairvaux, head of the Cistercian order, obtained from Pope Innocent VIII authority to celebrate mass pontifically with mitre, ring, and sandals. He was no longer a poor monk, leading a laborious and obscure life, but a magnificent and powerful personage, lord of five military orders, who sat in the parliament of Burgundy, on a level with the bishop.

'Annals of a Yorkshire Abbey' — William Grange, 1896

View from the S. transept. Left to right :- the archway of Huby's tower; Darnton's buttress; Huby's low arch. Both the latter were to support a problematic central tower.

THE INVENTORY OF SUCH THINGS AS WERE KEPT IN THE CHURCH OF FOUNTAINS

	£.	s.	d.
Nineteen chalices with pateyns, gilt, in all 495½ oz. and 3 dwts at 4s. 4d	107	7	10
Two white crewets, 12½ oz .... 3s. 2d.	1	19	7
Two crewets, gilt, 15½ oz .... 4s. 4d.	3	7	2
An ewer for the high altar, gilt, 12½ oz .... 3s. 2d.	1	19	7
A little chalice, without pateyn, gilt on the inside of the shell, 5 oz .... 3s. 8d.	0	18	4
A little chalice, without pateyn, gilt, 5¼ oz .... 4s. 4d.	1	2	9
A basin for the high altar, parcel gilt, 26½ oz .... 3s. 8d.	4	17	2
A schipe [skep or basket]^f for incense, of silver, and gilt, with a spoon, gilt, 25 oz ...... 3s. 8d.	4	11	8
Two candlesticks, gilt, for the high altar, 56 oz .... 4s. 4d.	12	2	8
A pair of censures, gilt, 42 oz .... 4s. 4d.	9	2	0
A cross-head silvered and gilt, with an image, 32 oz .... 4s. 4d.	6	18	8
A cruche-head,^g gilt, 46 oz .... 4s. 4d.	9	19	4
A staff of silver ungilt for the same cruche-head, 38½ oz .... 3s. 2d.	6	1	11
A piece of St. Anne's scalpe, set in silver, ungilt, 2½ oz .... 3s. 2d.	0	7	11
A pair of beads, silvered and gilt, 2½ oz .... 4s. 4d.	0	10	10
A mitre, having the edges of silver, and gilt, and set with round pieces of silver, white like pearl, and flowered of silver, and gilt in midward, 12 oz .... 4s. 4d.	2	12	0
A manse [or small shrine] with a rib of St. Lawrence, of silver gilt, 44 oz .... 4s. 4d.	9	10	8
A manse for Corpus Christi day, silver and gilt, 106 oz .... 4s. 4d.	22	19	4
A holy-water Fatt, with a strinkil [sprinkler] of silver, ungilt, 53 oz .... 3s. 2d.	8	7	10
A mitre of silver, gilt, and set with pearls and stone, 70 oz .... 4s. 4d.	15	3	4
A ring and buckle, silvered and gilt, set with pearls and stones, 4 oz .... 4s. 4d.	0	17	4
An image of St. James, of silver, and gilt, 64 oz .... s. 4d.	13	17	4
A cross, silvered and gilt, 1 oz	0	4	4
A grype-schill,^h with a covering, gilt, 37 oz .... 3s. 8d.	6	15	8
A cross of gold, set with stones, wherein is part of the holy cross, 14 oz .... £2. 3s. 0d.	30	2	0
A jewel of silver, and gilt, with a byrel,* 9½ oz .... 4s. 4d.	2	1	2
A cross, with a stone, of silver, and gilt, 20½ oz .... 4s. 4d.	4	8	10
A jewel, with a byrel, of silver, and gilt, 6½ oz .... 4s. 4d.	1	8	2
A foot of a cross, silvered and gilt, 9½ oz .... 4s. 4d.	2	1	2
A jewel, with a byrel and relict of silver, and gilt, 5 oz .... 4. 4d.	1	1	8
A box of silver, gilt within, beads gilt, 2½ oz .... 4. 4d.	0	10	10
An image of our Lady, in a case of silver, and gilt, 4½ oz .... 4s. 4d.	0	19	6
Two small jewels bound with bands of silver. The silver 3 oz .... 3s. 2d.	0	9	6
A little cross of silver, and gilt, 5½ oz . 4s. 4d.	1	3	10
A bruche† of silver, gilt, 3½ oz .... 4s. 4d.	0	15	2
Two pots of white, silvered, 6 oz ...... 3s. 2d.	0	19	0
Two great chrystal stones			
Two crewets of silver, gilt, 16½ oz ..... 4s. 4d.	3	11	6
A silver chalice, well gilt, 29 oz .... 4s. 6d.	6	10	6
A pateyn for the said chalice, of silver, gilt, 9½ oz .... 4s. 4d.	2	1	2
A pair of selors,^j of silver, gilt, 108 oz . 4s. 4d.	23	8	0
An image of our Lady, of silver, gilt, 104 oz .... 4s. 4d.	22	10	8
A silver cross, gilt, set with stones, 120 oz .... 4s. 4d.	26	0	0
A head of a cruche of silver, gilt, 100 oz .... 4s. 4d.	21	13	4
The staff of the cruche, gilt, 70 oz ..... 4s. 4d.	15	3	4
Two corpas [corporas] caps of cloth of gold ...			
A table for the high altar on principal days, with three images of silver, gilt, with heads and plate of silver, and some parts of gold, set with stones, valued at £90 or £94	90	0	0
	508	14	7

* beryl
† brooch

IN THE CUSTODY OF THE LORD ABBOT

	£.	s.	d.
A basin of silver, with a flower, gilt in the front, 56½ oz .... 3s. 5d.	9	13	1
A basin of silver, with a front gilt in the bottom, 54½ oz .... 3s. 5d.	9	5	4½
A pot, parcel gilt, 54 oz .... 3s. 6d.	9	9	0
Two silver ewers, 51 oz .... 3s. 4d.	8	10	0
A silver ewer, gilt about the edges, 25¼ oz .... 3s. 4d.	4	4	2
Eight standing pieces and covers, gilt, 278½ oz .... 4s. 4d.	60	6	10
Four flat pieces with covers, gilt, 101½ oz .... 4s. 4d.	21	19	10
A goblet covered and gilt, 19 oz .... 4s. 4d.	4	2	4
A cover of a piece, gilt, 12 oz .... 4s. 4d.	2	12	0
A flat piece and cover, not gilt, 48 oz . 3s. 5d.	8	4	0
A flat piece, the edges and front gilt, 16½ oz .... 3s. 6d.	2	17	9
A flat piece, skargells,^k gilt on the front and edges, 16 oz .... 3s. 6d.	2	16	0

		£.	s.	d.
Four gilt spoons, 7 oz	4s. 4d.	1	10	4
A serpent tongue, set in silver, 1¾ oz	3s. 5d.	0	5	11¾
Two flat pieces, not gilt, 11¼ oz	3s. 5d.	1	18	5¼
A little mass band and front, gilt, 5 oz	4s. 4d.	1	1	8
A chalice with the pateyn of silver, and gilt, 29 oz	4s. 4d.	6	5	3
Two crewets of silver, gilt, 11 oz	4s. 4d.	2	7	8
		157	10	1¼

[f] The thurible appears to be meant.
[g] Cruche : crook — a crosier.
[h] This seems to be a flagon; *schill* or *skeel* (derived from the French *escuelle*) being a northern provincialism for pail. The word may be rendered hand-skeel — a skeel which may be gripped or grasped by the hand, or that has a handle to it.
[i] Vessels for holding the salt, which, after being blessed, was mixed with the holy water.
[k] Not known.

THE STORES (STAURI) OF THE MONASTERY OF FOUNTAINS

Bulls	49	Bovets, or young steers	151
Oxen	536	Boviculæ, or young oxen whys[m]	142
Cows	738	Stirketts[m]	242
Heifers	151	Calves	347

Total, 2356.

STATE OF THE SHEEP

Hurt:[n] [rams]	50	Oves, or ewes	535
Multones, or wethers	421	Hogs, or sheep of one year old	320

Total, 1326

HORSES

Emiss: [breeding horses]	5	Equi, unius anni et ½	4
Equi ad stabul: domini abbatis	6	Fillies, unius anni et ½	11
Equi ad bigam: [carriage horses]	6	Pulli, or colts	17
Equæ	37		

Total, 86

SWINE

Boars	5	Porcul: young swine or porkings	17
Swine	9	Porcel: or suckings pigs	30
Porci	18		

Total, 79

OF THE DEMAINS OF THE MONASTERY

WHEAT

	Qrs.		Qrs.
At Morkar	36	At Swanlay	10
At Haddokstaynes	35	At Sutton	36

Total, 117

IN RYE

	Qrs.		Qrs.
At Brymbem	9	At Sutton	3

Total, 12

IN OATS

	Qrs.		Qrs.
At Morkar	30	At Sutton	40
At Haddokstaynes	24	At Brymbem	20
At Swanlay	20		

Total, 134

IN HAY

	Qrs.		Qrs.
At Morkar	60	At Sutton	20
At Haddokstaynes	40	At the monastery in the park	160
At Swanlay	12	At Brymbem	100

Total, 392

[m] *Whys, stirketts* — provincialisms signifying cattle from one and a half to two years old — the former female, the latter male.

Some of the possessions of Fountains Abbey surrendered to King Henry VIII in the chapter house, November 1539: given in 'Delineation of Fountains Abbey' — J. & H. S. Storer (circa 1830)

(In modern terms, the total value would have to be estimated in millions of pounds sterling.)

The west end of the Abbey at the height of summer.

Recovery and dissolution, 1436-1539

After these alarms and excursions, the rest of the fifteenth century proved to be a period of quiet consolidation and modest prosperity. The long and wise rule of the learned Abbot John Greenwell, despite his uncertain health, restored stability to the convent. Its numbers had now dwindled to thirty monks, with 117 servants and workmen, but the abbot was recognised as a great northern potentate and such granges as Brimham, Baldersby and Thorpe Underwoods were converted into country houses for his use. Abbot Greenwell and Abbot John Darnton, another just and capable administrator, were both Commissaries of the abbot of Cîteaux and Reformers of the Cistercian Order in England.

When Abbot Darnton died in 1495 he was succeeded by Marmaduke Huby, the best known and perhaps the greatest abbot of Fountains. Huby had already been a monk and obedientiary in the abbey for some thirty years when he was elected abbot, and to this long apprenticeship he added outstanding qualities of energy and decision. Although he is mainly remembered today as the builder of the great tower of the abbey church, during his thirty years as abbot he left his mark on practically every aspect of the affairs of his abbey and of his Order. As Reformer of the Cistercians he was described as a venerable father who stood like a golden and unbreakable column in his zeal for the Order, and under him the number of monks at Fountains, once as low as twenty-two, rose to fifty-two. He commissioned a revised inventory of the abbey's title deeds, he was an indefatigable repairer and rebuilder of the abbey's granges and chapels, and he was responsible for putting the Order's College of St. Bernard at Oxford on a firm footing.

Abbot Huby died in 1526, and by 1530 there were signs that his successor, Abbot William Thirsk, was not a prudent ruler. There is evidence that he was selling abbey timber without consulting the convent, although it would be unwise to place too much reliance on the more picturesque tales of his misdeeds, such as that which represents him taking jewels from the sacristy at dead of night to sell to a Cheapside goldsmith. The events that were the real cause of Abbot Thirsk's downfall started in 1533 when he questioned the authority of Thomas Cromwell, the king's chief minister, over the deposition of the abbot of Rievaulx. This marked him as a man unlikely to be amenable to the king's wishes, and when Dr Layton and Dr Legh, the royal agents for the visitation of the monasteries, arrived at Fountains in 1536, they forced the abbot to resign. Provided with a comfortable pension, he went to stay with his friend Abbot Sedbergh of Jervaulx.

The first year of his rule saw the outbreak of the rising in favour of the monasteries, known as the Pilgrimage of Grace. Abbot Bradley kept Fountains aloof from this, but his predecessor ex-Abbot Thirsk was less fortunate, for one of the incidents in the rising centred on Jervaulx Abbey where he had been staying. Along with his friend Abbot Sedbergh, Thirsk was accused of complicity in the insurrection, imprisoned in the Tower of London, and found guilty of treason at Westminster. In May 1537 he was hanged, drawn and quartered at Tyburn.

Fountains Abbey Guide Book
— R. Gilyard-Beer, 1970

Fountains Hall, at the West Gates, built by Sir Stephen Proctor (1598-1611) of stones dismantled from the Abbey infirmary.

The Abbey on a winter's day.

What the *Suppression* meant to the religious houses of the East Riding may be judged from the following letter, written in 1538 by a servant of Thomas Cromwell to his master:-

> Pleasythe your good Lordship to be advertysed. I have taken downe all the lead of Jervayse, and made itt in pecys of half-foders, which lead amounteth to the numbre of eighteen score and five foders, with thirty and foure foders, and a half, that were there before. And the said lead cannot be conveit, nor caryed unto the next sombre, for the ways in that contre are so foule, and deep, that no carrage can passe in wyntre. And as concerning the raising and taken downe the house, if itt be your Lordshipps pleasure I am minded to let itt stand to the Springs of the yere, by reason of the days are now so short it wolde be double charge to do itt now. And as concerning the selling of the bells, I cannot sell them above 15s, the hundreth, wherein I would gladly know your Lordshipps pleasor, whether I should sell after that price, or send them up to London. And if they be sent up surely the carriage wolbe costly frome that place to the water. And as for Byrdlington I have doyn nothing there as yet, but sparethe itt to March next, bycause the days now are so short, and from such tyme I trust shortly to dyspatche itt after such fashion that when all is fynished, I trust your Lordshipp shall think that I have bene no evyll howsbound in all such things, as your Lordshipp haith appoynted me to doo. And thus the Holy Ghost ever preserve your Lordshipp in honor. At York this fourteenth day of November by your most bounden beadsman.
> RICHARD BELLYCYS.

'The Story of the East Riding of Yorkshire'
Horace B. Browne 1912

The property was sold (after the dissolution in 1539) to Sir Richard Gresham in 1540, and in 1597 to Sir Stephen Proctor, who built Fountains Mall with stone obtained by pulling down part of the abbey building. Passing through many hands, including the Messenger family, it was sold in 1768 to William Aislabie of Studley, son of John Aislabie, who laid out the grounds of the park and constructed the artificial ponds. The united properties of Fountains and Studley came in 1808 into the possession of Miss Lawrence, grand-daughter of William Aislabie, who left them at her death to her kinsman the Right Hon. the Earl de Grey and Ripon, afterwards first Marquis of Ripon. On the death of his son in 1923, the properties were acquired by Mr. Clare Vyner, grand-nephew of the first Marquis.*

A pamphlet 'Fountains Abbey, the monks and the buildings' — Rev. A. W. Oxford, 1921

* The Abbey was bought in 1966, along with the Studley Royal Estate, by the West Riding Council and in 1983 was purchased by the National Trust. English Heritage (Historic Buildings and Monuments Commission for England) are responsible for its preservation and restoration.

A stream in Applegarths running underground.

The Skell in flood after a thaw.

Glory be to God on high. On Sundays and festival days on which we work.

Glory be to God on high, and on earth peace to men of good will. We praise thee, we bless thee, we adore thee, we glorify thee. We give thee thanks for thy great glory. O Lord God, King of Heaven, God the Father Almighty. O Lord Jesus Christ the only-begotten Son. O Lord God, Lamb of God, Son of the Father. Thou who takest away the sins of the world, have mercy on us. Thou who takest away the sins of the world, receive our prayer. Thou who sittest at the right hand of the Father, have mercy on us. For thou only art Holy, thou only art Lord, thou only art Most High, O Jesus Christ, with the Holy Ghost, in the glory of God, the Father. Amen.

The Credo is always sung together.

I Believe in one God, the Father Almighty, Maker of heaven and earth, of all things visible and invisible. And in one Lord Jesus Christ, the only-begotten Son of God. And born of the Father before all ages. God of God, light of light, true God of true God. Begotten, not made, consubstantial with the Father: by whom all things were made. Who for us men, and for our salvation descended from heaven. And was incarnate by the Holy Ghost of the Virgin Mary: and was made man. Was crucified also for us: suffered under Pontius Pilate and was buried. And the third day he rose again, according to the Scriptures. And ascended into heaven: sitteth at the right hand of the Father. And again he shall come with glory, to judge the living and the dead: of whose kingdom there shall be no end. And in the Holy Ghost, the Lord and lifegiver; who proceedeth from the Father and the Son. Who together with the Father and the Son is adored and conglorified: who spake by the prophets. And one, holy, Catholic and Apostolic Church. I confess one baptism for the remission of sins. And I expect the resurrection of the dead. And the life of the world to come. Amen.

Part of a Cistercian Missal, Paris 1516 — inscribed 'Sold in Paris, Cîteaux and Clairvaux'.

13th century tesselated tile-work at the high altar: though upon the site of the altar, the tiles were probably laid in the 18th century from the remains of an original paving in this area.

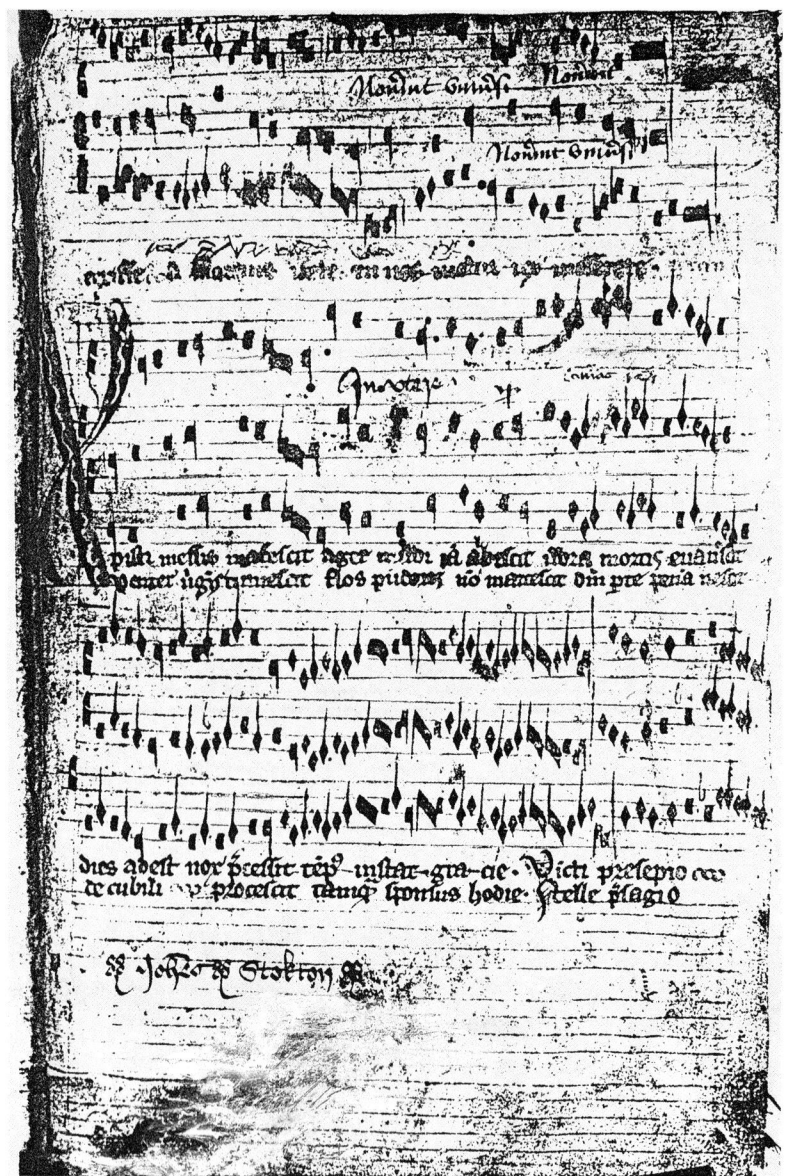

'Hymn to the Virgin', 14th C. polyphony in a Fountains Abbey manuscript book — by courtesy of the British Museum Library, (see below).

Most of the large musical manuscripts of which we have today some indirect record or even some direct remains suffered destruction during the Reformation. However, such planned destructive policies were pursued not only in that period but also, if for different reasons, in the monasteries of the fourteenth and fifteenth centuries. Musical manuscripts considered outdated at the time were cut up and used in bindings of non-musical books. Well concealed as fly-leaves or protective covers of fascicles, they weathered the storm of centuries and can now be removed from their hiding places, many of which may as yet have remained undiscovered. It is mainly from such mutilated and isolated leaves that we, like a palaeontologist who reconstructs from a few scattered bones an extinct species, can piece together a fairly comprehensive picture of medieval English music. Although the fragments may be small and not necessarily revealing in themselves, taken together they sketch the outline of a large body of music and give us evidence in much the same manner as the visible part of an iceberg does of its total dimensions.

'Studies in Medieval and Renaissance Music' — Manfred Bukofzer, 1950

The music manuscript consists of four leaves of parchment written on both sides, measuring 8⅞ x 5⁷⁄₁₆ used as fly-leaves in a miscellaneous manuscript book. The book and its contents (once in the library at Ripley Castle, later in Fountains Abbey museum, and now in the British Library) are said to have belonged to Fountains Abbey together with other books in the same collection. This origin is confirmed in evidence in the book itself: at the top of folio 4 the words 'lib ace de ffot' appear in a medieval hand and ink.

Analogies with similar sources, for example with music manuscript discovered in the binding of a memorandum book of Fountains Abbey (mid 15th century) by Dr. Bertram Schofield in the British Museum, make it probable that the complete music manuscript from which these four fly-leaves were taken and used for binding purposes, originated at Fountains and had fallen into disuse by the early 15th century . . . The music and handwriting may be assigned to the first third of the 14th century.

H. K. Andrews & Thurston Dart — 'Music and Letters' journal, Jan 1958

The nave of the church, W. end.

Tame chaffinches eating crusts on the cafe table.

The black monks (Benedictines) reproached the Cistercians with wearing a garment fit only for a time of joy, whilst the monastic state was one of penitence. But the white monks answered, that the life of a monk was not only one of penitence, but was like that of the angels, and therefore they wore white garments to show the spiritual joy of their hearts. And notwithstanding their coarse bread and hard beds, there was a cheerfulness about the Cistercians which may, in a great measure be traced to what we should now call a sympathy with nature. Their life lay out of doors, amongst vineyards and cornfields; their monasteries, as their names testify were mostly situated in sequestered valleys, and were by a law of the order, never in towns but in the country. From their constant meditations as they worked, they acquired a habit of joining their recollections of Scripture to natural objects — hence, also, the love for the Song of Solomon, which is evident in the early ascetic writers of the order.

'A Concise History of the Cistercian Order'
— a Cistercian monk, 1852

v 10 My beloved spoke, and said unto me, Rise up, my love, my fair one, and come away.

v 11 For lo, the winter is past, the rain is over and gone;

v 12 The flowers appear on the earth; the time of the singing of birds is come . . .

'Song of Solomon', Ch. 2, v.10 11 12 (Old Testament)

'I meditated on the Word of God, and the fields and the forests taught me its secret meaning: the oaks and the beeches were my masters.'

St. Bernard of Clairvaux (1091-1153)

A peaceful spring day at the Abbey.

BONUM EST NOS ESSE QUIA MOMO VIVIT PURIUS,
CADIT RARIUS, SURGIT VELOCIUS, INCEDIT CAUTIUS
QUIESCIT SECURIUS, MORITUR FELICIUS,
PURGATUR CITIUS, PROEMIATUR COPIOSIUS.

It is good for us to be here because a man lives more cleanly,
falls more rarely, rise more swiftly, proceeds more carefully,
rests more securely, dies more happily,
is purified more quickly, is rewarded more generously.

> Latin inscription found on the walls of Cistercian houses — attributed to St. Bernard.

Agnus Dei, qui tollis peccata mundi,
Dona eis requiem sempiternam.

O Lamb of God, that takest away the sins of the
 world.
Grant them eternal rest.

Glossary of Words Unexplained in the Book

abbot .... Latin *abbas* 'abbot' from Syriac *abba* 'father'; thus the head of an abbey or monastery.

aisle .... Latin *āla* 'wing'. The two aisles in a church are divided from the nave by pillars. The imagery of the bird is obvious.

aumbry or ambry Med. Latin *armārium* 'cupboard', from Latin *arma* 'arms, tools'. A recess in a wall to house the vessels and linen used in the Eucharist.

bovate .... Lat. *bōs, bovis* 'an ox'; a measure of land, variable but between 8 and 16 acres; it is also known as an oxgang — i.e. an area workable by an ox.

bracket .... see under 'corbel'

capital .... Lat. *caput* 'head'; the diminutive *capitulum* is the 'head of a column'.

carucate .... Lat. *carrūca* 'a plough' — thus a plough's worth, equivalent to eight bovates, say a 100 acres: a taxable measure.

cellarium (and cellarer) Lat. *cella* 'a store-room' or 'granary hut'; Greek *kalīa*. The root meaning is 'to conceal', indicating safety of food in times of invasion. In a monastery it is the place for provisions. The cellarer is the monk in charge.

chamberlain .. Greek *kamára* 'anything with a vaulted or arched roof'; ling is Germanic suffix. The officer in charge of a monarch's private apartments — in a monastery of the dormitory clothes and general comfort.

chantry .... Lat. *cantare* 'to sing'. An altar or chapel for the purpose of singing masses for the repose of the soul after death.

chapter-house Old French *chapiter*, from Lat. *capitulum*, 'small division of a book, chapter'. Such a chapter of the Rule of St. Benedict was read after mass, and the place in which it was read acquired the name.

choir .... Greek *khorós* 'dancing in a ring — a festive dance in a ring to the honour of the Gods'. In the present 'choir', the festival is vocal only; it is the area between nave and sanctuary, east of the rood-screen, that houses the singers. It is often called the chancel.

Cistercian ...... *Cistercium* is the Latin word for the French *Cîteaux* — the marshy locality of the first monastery of the Order. Cîteaux is from the local French dialect *cistels* 'reeds'.

compline .... Lat. *complēta* 'completed'; the last service of the day.

conversi .... Lat. *conversus* 'turned about'. Conversi were lay-men who had turned from the service of the world to the service of God — (see lay-brother).

corbel .... French *corbel*, from Lat. *corvus* 'raven'. A block of stone projecting from a wall resembling the raven's beak; it is a support taking the strain of a beam or vault.

day-stairs .... the stairs giving access to the dormitory by day. At Fountains, the monks' day-stairs are in the cloister and the lay-brothers' on the outer wall of the cellarium.

dole .... Old Engl. *dal* 'part, division' — so, 'that which is apportioned'.

dormitōrii necessāria ... the reredorter or sanitary block: literally 'that which is necessary to the dormitory' — another euphemism among many for the sanitary arrangements.

dorter .... An abbreviation of Lat. *dormitorium* 'sleeping room' through O. Fr. *dorteur*. (Lat. *dormire* 'to sleep').

farmery .... variant on infirmary.

frater .... Another form of refectory. Frater is not connected with its apparent meaning of 'brother' but is an abbreviation, from Lat. *refreitor*, a version of *refectōrium,* 'refectory'.

Galilee porch .. Lat. *galeria*, 'a long porch'; the porch at the west end of the church. It is possible that the word comes directly from the biblical Galilee. The connection then would be with the weekly Sunday festival of the Resurrection, the porch being the last Station in the procession of dignitary and followers, as Christ was followed by the disciples into Galilee after the Resurrection (J. T. Fowler). There are other interpretations.

grange .... Med. Latin *granea* 'barn for grain', from *grānum* 'grain'. A collection of buildings connected with this, together with living quarters. Cistercian monastic granges, mostly based on sheep farming were run by lay-brothers.

hospitium (hospitia pl.) ... Latin word meaning 'hospitality' from *hospes*, 'guest'. Thus the guest-house of a monastery (French 'hospice' is sometimes used).

Lady Chapel ... A name for the Chapel of the Nine Altars — because of its consecration to the Virgin Mary.

lauds — Lat. *laudāre* 'to praise'; the office at day-break. It was counted the first of the seven canonical hours of the Benedictine day, and was originally called matins.

mandatum — see under 'maundy'.

matins — Lat. *Mātūta*, the goddess of morning; the first service of the day lasting an hour or more. It was originally called vigils, that is a nocturnal watch.

maundy — Old French *mandé*, from Lat. *mandātum* 'command'; with reference to Christ's command in St. John 13 that since he had set the example the disciples should wash one another's feet. Thus, a symbolic act of humility among the brethren — also seen in washing the feet of the poor.

minutor — Latin, a technical term for the physician or monastery official qualified to let blood, — 'he who makes smaller' from the root *min* 'small'.

misericord — Lat. *misereri* 'to have compassion for' — and *cor* 'heart'. The term is usually applied to the ledge on the underside of hinged seats in the choir stalls affording relief from standing during service. In the present context it also applies to a room connected with the infirmary where certain indulgences were allowed for ill or elderly monks, e.g. the eating of meat.

muniment room — Lat. *mūnīre* 'to defend'; a room in a monastery where title-deeds, documents, etc. were kept, also acting as a safe-deposit for those outside the monastery.

mitre — Greek *mītra* 'head-band'; a conical cap divided by a cleft worn by bishops, and by some abbots of monasteries by permission of the Pope.

nave — Lat. *nāvis* 'ship'. The ship is the Church of Christ in which souls are saved from the waters of life. The nave is the secular part of the church as opposed to the sanctuary or holy part within the altar rails, W. and E. respectively.

nones — Lat. *nōnus* 'ninth'. The office celebrating the ninth hour, 3pm, counting 6am as prime.

parlour — Lat. *parlāre* 'to talk'; the small room in a monastery where essential conversation was allowed.

pentise (or pentice) — Lat. *appendicium* 'an appendage'; the popular form is 'penthouse'; a sloping roof attached to a wall forming a shelter or passage way.

precentor — Lat. *pre* 'before, forwards' and *cantor* 'singer'; the leader of the singing. In a monastery he was also librarian and organised processions and church services.

presbytery — Greek *presbutērion* 'the place of the presbyters', from *presbúteros* 'elder'. The sanctuary or eastern end of the chancel.

pier — Low Lat. *pera*, from Greek *pétra* 'rock'; a mass of stone supporting an arch or roof, as opposed to a column, though the word is loosely used for a column or pillar of great size.

piscina — Lat. *piscina* 'fish-pond', from *piscis* 'fish': a stone basin in a niche in the wall of a church near the altar, used by the priest for cleansing the chalice and his own hands, at the Eucharist. (The symbolism of the fish is frequently found in the New Testament.)

prime — Eccl. Lat. *prīma (hora)* 'first hour'; the office sung at the first hour of day, 6am at the equinoxes.

prior — Latin base meaning 'first'; the first in rank under the abbot in a monastery.

pulpitum — Latin meaning 'platform, scaffold'. A stone screen with a gallery often housing the organ (marks on the piers at Fountains indicate it was on the S. side), and also a place from which readings were made during services.

rebus — Lat. *rēbus* 'things'; an enigmatic representation of a name by things or pictures found in heraldry and on monuments and tombs.

refectory — Lat. *refectio* 'a re-making, re-freshment', from *reficere* 'to re-make', i.e. with the help of food.

reredorter — Old French *arere* 'at the back' and *dorter*, abbreviation of dormitory from Lat. *dormire* 'to sleep'; thus behind the sleeping quarters, a euphemism for the sanitary block.

retro-choir — Latin *retro* 'at the back, behind'. Usually this is an area behind and E. of the choir and high altar — a processional way. At Fountains, it refers to an area at the extreme W. end of the monks' church, which was the lower entrance through the pulpitum into the choir. It was used during offices by the old and infirm.

sacristy — Lat. *sacer* 'holy'; the room adjoining a church where liturgical vessels were kept. The monk responsible for their care was the sacrist, who was also keeper of books and vestments. The word sacristy is loosely used for vestry.

scapular — Lat. *scapula* 'shoulder blade'; a garment with a hood but no sleeves, used for working.

springer — The lowest stone of an arch in a vaulted roof or arcade — that from which it springs.

sext — Lat. *sextus* 'sixth'; the office celebrating the sixth house — noon, counting 6am as prime.

tesselated tilework — Lat. *tessella*, 'small piece of stone': such pieces were used for mosaic work in pavings.

tierce — Lat. *tertius* 'third'; the office celebrating the third hour, 9am, counting 6am as prime.

undercroft ..... croft is related to Latin *crupta* 'crypt'; a vaulted chamber under a main room in a church, or monastic buildings.

vespers .... Lat. *vesper* 'evening'; the office celebrated at evening, variable.

vestry .... Lat. *vestis* 'clothing'; the room adjoining a church where liturgical vestments are keptd and put on. The word is loosely used for sacristy (vide).

vill .... A unit of civil as opposed to manorial administration — a feudal territorial division.

warming house ... a room with fires used in the cold season, between Nov 1st and Easter; the room was something of a common room, used for such occasions as blood letting or tonsuring.

expressions used in the deeds:

'granted in pure and perpetual alms', means granted in exchange for prayers given in perpetuity.

'quit and free of all land service', means free of obligation to give service or work of any kind.

'toft and croft', means a homestead and its surrounding land.

'fee of a knight', means the fee or price for being made a knight; someone given land by the crown would agree, along with his retainers, to perform military service.

'appurtenances, liberties and easements', means respectively all extra buildings, properties owned under the jurisdiction of the crown, and rights of way.

A model in the museum reconstructing the Abbey as it may have been circa 1250. The view is from the east end, with the infirmary and its buildings in the foreground.

List of literary sources quoted. An asterisk denotes permission kindly granted from the publisher or copyright owner.

* The Cathedral Builders — Jean Gimpel (Evergreen Books Ltd., London, 1961).
* The Waters of Siloe — Thomas Merton (Sheldon Press, 1950).
* The Story of England — Arthur Bryant (Collins, Sons & Co., London, 1953).
* English Historical Documents — J. C. Douglas & A. W. Greenaway (Eyre and Spottiswood, Andover, 1959).
* The Fountains Story — A. M. Wilkinson (Harrison Ltd., Ripon, 1957).
* The Monastic Orders in England — D. Knowles (Camb. Un. Press, Cambridge, 1940).
* Fountains Abbey, a poem — E. K. Ellis (Camb. Un. Press, Cambridge, 1948).
* Medieval Chantries and Chantry Chapels — G. H. Cook (J. M. Dent & Sons Ltd., London, 1963).
* Fountains Abbey Guide Book — R. Gilyard Beer (London, 1970).
* The Ruins of Fountains Abbey — Rev. A. W. Oxford (Oxford Un. Press, Oxford, 1910).
* Fountains Abbey (a pamphlet) — Rev. A. W. Oxford (Harrison, Ripon, 1921).
* The English Abbey — F. H. Crossley (Batsford Ltd., London, 1935).
* English Abbeys — Hugh Braun (Faber & Faber Ltd., 1971).
* The Life of Ailred of Rievaux — Walter Daniel (ed. and trans. by M. Powicke, Clarendon Press, 1950).
* Thomas Merton on St. Bernard — (Cistercian Publications, Kalamzoo, Michigan, U.S.A., 1950).
* Fountains Abbey Lease Book — Yorks. Archaeological Society Record Series, Vol 140, 1981.
* The Deanery of Craven — T. D. Whitaker (The Craven Herald, Skipton, 1879).
* A History of Nidderdale — ed. Bernard Jennings (Advertiser Press Ltd., Huddersfield).
* Studies in Renaissance and Medieval Music — Manfred Bukofzer (W. W. Norton & Co., New York, 1950).
* Music and Letters Journal — H. K. Andrews and Thurston Dart (OUP, Oxford, 1958).
* The Rule of Benedict (525-550) — Burns and Oates, 1886.

English Monasteries — A. Hamilton Thompson (Cambridge Un. Press, 1923).
Yorkshire Archaeological and Topographical Journal, Vol. 10, 1886.
An Ecclesiastical History of Yorkshire — Dr. Burton, 1757.
Murray's Handbook for Travellers in Yorkshire — 1882.
Highways and Byways in Yorkshire — Arthur Norway (McMillan and Co. Ltd., 1923).
Fountains Abbey — George Hodges (Dutton and Co., New York, 1904).
The Story of the Founding of Fountains Abbey (The Fountains Chronicle) — Hugh of Kirkstall, 1207.
A Guide to Ripon and Fountains Abbey — J. R. Walbran (Johnson & Co., 1856).
Annals of a Yorkshire Abbey — William Grange (Ackrill, Harrogate, 1896).
The Ruined Abbeys of Yorkshire — W. C. Lefroy (Seeley & Co. 1891).
Studies in Renaissance and Medieval Music — Manfred Bukofzer (Dent, 1950).
Memorials of Fountains Abbey — Surtees Society, Vol. 130 1918.
Memorials of Fountains Abbey — Surtees Society, Vol. 67 1876.
Memorials of Fountains Abbey — Surtees Society, Vol. 42 1862.
A History of the Work of the Cistercians in Yorkshire — F. A. Mullin (Catholic University of America, 1932).
Yorkshire Archaeological Journal (Jervaux Abbey) — St. John Hope and H. Brakspear, Vol. 21 1911.
Yorkshire Archaeological Journal (The Cistercian Order) — J. T. Micklethwaite, Vol. 15 1900.
Yorkshire Archaeological Journal (Fountains Abbey) St. John Hope, Vol. 15 1898.
Yorkshire Archaeological Journal, Vol. 29 1929.
Chartulary of the Cistercian Abbey of Fountains — Wm. T. Lancaster, 1915.
Monks and Monasteries — Samuel Fox (Burns, 1845).
Lake District History — W. G. Collingwood (Titus Wilson, Kendal, 1928).
The Story of the East Riding of Yorkshire — H. B. Browne (Brown and Sons, Hull, 1912).
Collecteanea Archaeologica — British Architectural Association, 1871.
Delineations of Fountains Abbey — J. & H. S. Storer (Longman & Co. circa 1830).
The Cistercian Fathers — Lives and Legends — trans. H. Collins (Richardson, Dublin, 1874).
Cistercian Ritual and Uses — Paris, 1689.
Cistercian Missal — inscribed 'sold in Paris, Citeuax and Clairvaux', 1516.
A Concise History of the Cistercian Order — a Cistercian monk, 1852.
Early Yorkshire Charters — Yorks. Arch. Soc. Rec. Ser., Vol VII.
Monastic Chancery Proceedings — Yorks. Arch. Soc. Rec. Serv., Vol 88 1934.
Sixty Centuries of Health and Physick — S. G. Bloxland Stubbs & E. W. Bligh (Samson Low, Marston & Co. 1931).

N.B. Every effort has been made to trace owners of copyright of more recent works. In one or two cases it has not been possible, but if the error should have been mine or there has been an inadvertent omission, I offer apologies and will redress the wrong in future editions. H.W.

Index to Photographs

abbot's house, 37, 125.
Applegarths, 184; east Applegarths, 118; west Applegarths, 7, 32.

bakehouse, 30, 104, 114.
Bewerley chapel, 154-5.
bridge (12th C.), 54, 83.

cellarer's office, 21, 113, 117.
cellarium, 12, 21, 115.
Chapel of the Nine Altars, 8, 38, 44, 69, 70, 71, 73-5, 139, 171.
Chapel of St Michael, How Hill, 165.
chapter house, 9, 46, 48-9, 51-2, 90-91, 167.
choir, 63.
cloister, 11, 57, 60, 93, 103-4, 149.
crossing, 63.

Darnton's east window, 174; buttress, 177.
day-stairs, 11, 42, 60, 121, 158.

Fountains Fell, 153.
Fountains Hall, 182.
fishpond, 118.

Galilee porch, 142.
gatehouse, 15, 147-8.
guest houses, 54, 80-1, 148; east guest house, 82-3, 158; west guest house, 76, 78.

high altar, 187.
Huby's arch, 64, 177; tower, 41, 175-7.

infirmary, 34, 133-4, 136.
    cellar, 130, 138, 139.
    chapel, 140.
    hall, 137.
    kitchen, 120, 140.
    passage, 57, 103, 134.

Kilnsey Old Hall, 152.
kitchen, 93, 103-4, 106, 109-10.

lavatory, 103, 130.
lay-brothers' day-stairs, 42, 113, 121.
    dormitory, 18-19, 21, 104.
    infirmary, 19-20, 121.

range, 12, 21, 94, 100, 111, 127, 145.
refectory, 21, 100, 111.
reredorter, 17, 19, 54, 122.
malthouse, 104, 107.
mill, 35.
mill bridge, 59.
misericord, 29, 134.
monks' dormitory, 26, 42, 56, 85-6, 89, 91, 157.
    refectory, 93, 99-101, 103-6, 166.
    reredorter, 37, 124.
muniment room, 85, 105, 157-8.
museum, 143.

nave, 4, 46, 61, 66, 68, 93, 189.
night-stairs, 19, 91.
north aisle, 43, 66.
northern industrial building: see bakehouse.

parlour, 12, 48, 131.
Pen-y-ghent, 153.
precinct walls, 118, 128, 147.
presbytery, 41, 64, 67, 69, 73.
prison, 37.

rebus, 170, 171.

sacristy, 45, 89.
river Skell, 27, 34, 100, 134, 185.
south aisle, 2, 5, 66, 68.
southern industrial buildings: see malthouse.
south transept, 56, 64, 89, 90-1, 104.
    chapels, 45, 65.
Studley Royal, 68.

tesselated tile-work, 187.
treasury, 90.
tunnels, 127, 136.

undercroft, 26, 57, 85-6.

warming house, 85, 93, 95, 97, 103, 157-8.
west face, 163, 192.
west gates, 182.

Yew trees, 24.